I attended the same church as Gerrie Mills and her family for a time during my childhood, but I know her now through two of her sons. Suffice it to say, they were raised well. I also know all about her now through the pages of her memoir, and I recommend it highly. It's not only hilarious, it's also a love story. But at its core, it's a good, old-fashioned salvation story. And it doesn't get any better than that.

—JERRY B. JENKINS
NOVELIST
CO-AUTHOR OF THE BESTSELLING *LEFT BEHIND* SERIES

Gerrie's story of her search for God inspired me deeply. It is truly thrilling for me to read the account of how a Jewish girl found her Messiah. Gerrie's new book *Oy Vey! Such A Deal* is a moving journal of her life's adventures and it is a magnetic book from cover to cover.

—PAT BOONE

My husband and I had visited ten churches to find one where we could embrace the teaching as well as the people. When Gerrie greeted us at the door I was struck with her warmth. She acted as if I were the only person in the room. She and Clyde invited us to brunch that day. Gerrie is so refreshing with her authenticity, humor, and deep spirituality. I had once heard that a church reflects the personality of the Pastor's wife. It is true in this case—Gerrie and Clyde both exude a Christ-likeness that draws you in. Oh yes, and she sparkles, too.

—NANCY NASH-LUND, MA
MARRIAGE AND FAMILY THERAPIST

Faith in an unchanging faithful God is what Gerrie is all about. A God she found to be absolutely reliable as she dared to trust Him as Savior, Lord, and Friend. As a fellow Pastor's wife I can tell you the parsonage is the place to find out the reality of God and the transforming power of His presence. If you don't you'll never make it in the ministry. With wit and wisdom Gerrie takes us with her to see the sense of trusting Him with our lives: the joys and sorrows, too.

—JILL BRISCOE

Gerrie Hyman Mills

OY VEY!
SUCH A DEAL

GERRIE HYMAN MILLS

A STRANG COMPANY

Oy Vey! Such a Deal by Gerrie Mills
Published by Creation House
A Strang Company
600 Rinehart Road
Lake Mary, Florida 32746
www.creationhouse.com

Unless otherwise marked, Scripture quotations are from the Holy Bible, New Living Translation, copyright © 1996. Used by permission of Tyndale House Publishers, Inc., Wheaton, IL 60189. All rights reserved.

All Scripture quotations marked kjv are from the King James Version of the Bible.

The names of some of the persons mentioned in this book have been changed in order to preserve their anonymity.

Many of the colloquial Yiddish passages appearing in this book were verified at the Yiddish In America Web site: http://www .koshernosh.com/in-ameri.htm.

Cover design by Marvin Eans

Library of Congress Control Number: 2007936687
International Standard Book Number: 978-1-59979-264-4

First Edition

07 08 09 10 11 — 9 8 7 6 5 4 3 2 1
Printed in the United States of America

Contents

DEDICATIONS

From Gerrie...

This book is dedicated to my husband, Clyde. Your
charm, humor, and wisdom have kept me loving and
laughing throughout my life. Who would have thought
our tender love would grow into the adoring adventure
we have enjoyed for more than five decades? Each day I
watch you put your heart and soul into the caring things
you do, and I am so thankful that you are my husband,
my pastor, and my best friend.

For Gerrie...

Mom,

I'm convinced if the Bible were written today, God would
have featured you as one of the main characters, perhaps
even titled a book of the Bible after you—"Giddel Faggee
Hymovictch" (your full name in Hebrew).

You truly are one-of-a-kind, and there is no way to
describe what life with you is like. The stories in this
book are like taking a photo of a beautiful California
sunset—there's no possible way to capture the over-
whelming feeling it leaves you with. But we are thrilled
that you finally collected these precious memories into a
book. We will cherish these pages forever.

On behalf of your children, grandchildren, and future great grandchildren, we are so blessed to have such a wonderful Mom who is our passionate prayer warrior, "self-appointed advisor," shopping pal, fashion consultant, and price negotiator! We love sharing our lives with you—laughing, crying, eating chocolate pudding, and watching you wheel and deal! It is an honor to call the most inspirational person we know "Mom" and "Best Friend"! We love you!

Your daughter,
Lori Anne
(for the entire family)

Acknowledgments

For my dear friend and developmental editor, Cindy Cutts, whose persistent encouragement helped me get this book written. We have become the closest of friends, as you often do when you work together for months. We prayed over every line in the book. Cindy now knows what it is like to live as a pastor's wife; she has been at my side as I have attempted to both fulfill my role as Clyde's helpmate and write my book to encourage others in their walk of faith. Cindy's ability to capture my thoughts, and especially my expressions, still has me astounded. The only thing she hasn't accomplished—yet—is an unlimited love for chocolate pudding.

My gratitude to Susan Koster for her time and expertise in helping me create my book.

What a pleasure it has been to make such quality friends at Creation House under the godly leadership of Allen Quain. I just adore your quick thinking and your helpful spirit. You are amazing and I am very grateful for everything you have done to make my book a reality.

For my editor and newest dear friend, Robert Caggiano, a real mensch, whose editorial chutzpah helped me bring out the message of my book. Your sharp wit is a gift, and we laughed together every day for months, working to make my book as enjoyable for readers as it was to produce with you. I will miss our daily routine—not least of which your zeal for each new Yiddish expression I taught you—until I finish writing book number two. *Zay Gezunt,* my friend.

I want to thank my grandson David, who is a gifted photographer and, in fact, captured the portrait on the cover of this book. I admire him and am thankful for his growing love for his Jewish heritage, for Israel, and his grandmother.

INTRODUCTION

GERRIE IS THE love of my life. Together we are a team and I respect and honor her ministry, especially since we were both called by the Lord on the very same day. While Gerrie supports my work as a pastor, she is also out there doing her own work in ways that I never could.

I admire her passion and zest for life. She's artistic and creative and uses those gifts to share Jesus with just about anybody who will listen. Gerrie's world isn't just in color, it's in vibrant, fluorescent color and she adds that color to individual lives in every encounter.

All our married lives, Gerrie has been looking for a bargain. She negotiates every transaction she can. Her ability to find a "good deal" was realized best when she accepted eternal life through Jesus many years ago. Since then, Gerrie has offered this same great deal to many others who have eagerly accepted.

Gerrie's *chutzpah*, coupled with her big, loving heart, work well together in her commitment to serving the Lord. Our lives together are a daily adventure, and I am so grateful to have had her as my trusted colleague in ministry and my devoted partner in life. So, hold on to your hat, you are in for a wild ride as you read, *Oy Vey! Such A Deal!*

—CLYDE A. MILLS, Pastor

FOREWORD

"**L**ORD, PLEASE HELP me find believers back home who will accept my over-the-top personality and newfound faith." This was my prayer as a new Christian. Two weeks later God answered, when I walked into a country church nestled in a grove of pine trees, near Quincy, Michigan, and met the fabulous, flamboyant, and fun-loving pastor's wife, Gerrie Hyman Mills.

Our outrageous and gregarious personalities instantaneously bonded. Once I met the passionate Gerrie, I knew I'd found an exciting new church home. Gerrie's boldness and gift of creative evangelism inspired me to be true to the personality God designed for me in Psalm 139.

Gerrie never dressed like a pastor's wife and she didn't talk like a traditional pastor's wife. But people loved her, and that gave me encouragement to be myself. Gerrie accepted me just as I was and didn't try to squelch my eccentric personality. She encouraged me to use it.

After an invigorating session of aerobics in the church gym next door, Gerrie would gather all the young girls into her kitchen to bake chocolate chip cookies. As we ate ice cream and nibbled on the cookies, she would teach us to recognize how God was working in our lives. There were so many girls in attendance that we sat on the floor as Gerrie taught us how to share that excitement with others. I remember that

Gerrie always chose to sit on the floor, with her back against her refrigerator.

God used Gerrie as a "second mom" to encourage my sanguine personality. That continued as I became an "out-of-the-box" public school teacher, inspirational speaker, sign language dramatist, wife, and mother.

This year when God opened the door for me to be Mrs. Michigan American 2007, one of the first people I called is the true queen in my life, Gerrie Hyman Mills. Gerrie's crowning influence in my life has been "such a deal for me!"

—LAURA LOVEBERRY

Laura Loveberry was crowned Mrs. Michigan America 2007. She graduated magna cum laude from Ball State University with a BS in Art Education. Laura is a public school art teacher, an inspirational speaker, and also works as an interpreter for the deaf. She lives in Quincy, Michigan, with her husband Mark and their two children, Markus, fourteen, and Madison, nine.

Chapter 1

MEIN *SHEYNE MEYDELE*

T HOUGH MUCH OF my childhood is blurry to me now, I can recall a safe and loving home; one where I was loved and adored, and to a degree, sheltered from the harsh reality that outside the walls of that home, there were people who hated the Jewish community. I was growing up during the height of World War II and would soon find out that the hatred for my people would reach farther than Europe; it would come all the way to my little world of Kalamazoo, Michigan.

I first experienced prejudice in kindergarten as I ventured outside of my home and walked several blocks down Lay Boulevard to Washington Elementary School. There was a group of brothers who would walk along the opposite side of the street and yell, "Dirty Jew, dirty Jew, we're in this war, because of you!" The brothers were in the fifth- and sixth-grades and looked like giants to me. I was confused and terrified at their angry insults. I had never done anything to them, and yet they hated me.

As wintertime came, the boys would put stones in their snowballs and throw them at me as I walked past. Their jeers and taunts terrified me and every day as I walked I shed tears, which seemed to encourage their ridicule. Sometimes Mother would walk with me, and then they would leave us alone, but my eyes and my heart began to understand that there was something different about who we were.

It was the same routine, over and over, throughout elementary school. I would find myself persecuted in unsuspecting situations. I still recall the heartbreak of one such incident. Once when I was in the second grade, I had been invited to a very special birthday party by a pretty little girl named Sally. I was so excited and proudly carried my birthday present to school, all wrapped up in pink polka dot paper and white satin ribbon. It was a long day in the classroom as all the little girls were excited for the day to end so we could all go to the party. Finally, at the end of the day, as the children gathered to go to Sally's house, she timidly came up to me. Sadly she informed me that I couldn't come to her party.

I was devastated. I was still so innocent. Through my tears I asked her, "But why not, Sally?" She answered, "I can't tell you. My daddy just said you couldn't." And then I knew. I asked her hesitantly, "Is it because I'm Jewish?" She looked down, averting her eyes, and whispered, "Yes."

I recall another instance of discrimination when I went to go sliding downhill with the neighbor children. When I got there, they wouldn't let me play with them and told me to go home. "We don't like Jews!" they all shouted. I went home crying. When I told Mother what had happened, she was so upset that she grabbed my father's slippers to go over there and give them a piece of her mind. I was mortified! It was bad enough that my schoolmates shunned me for being Jewish. What would they think seeing Mother stomping up the hill wearing Daddy's bedroom slippers in the snow?

In spite of the opposition we faced as children, I learned to be proud of my heritage and found comfort in it. Mother and Daddy instilled a deep respect for the sacrifices made by my grandfather, Sam Berman, who had escaped the Czar in Russia during the Pogroms and immigrated to the United States as young man. When he escaped Minsk, Belarus (then western Russia), to New York, he spent weeks crawling on his stomach during the night and sleeping during the day when it was too dangerous to travel.

My sister Bedonna and I were taught that it was during a time in history when our people the Jews were being persecuted for no other reason than for being Jewish. It caused me to cherish my ancestry and the relationships I had with my family and with the rest of the Jewish community of Kalamazoo, but I especially cherished my relationship with Daddy.

My father was the dearest man, to all those who knew him. He was a good provider for our family with a career in sales. For Daddy, work was his love. He occasionally played golf, but he wasn't very good at it. I remember him being a voracious reader, and he loved history, current events, and music.

He adored my mother and treated her well, despite her domineering personality. My mother's will was stronger than most, perhaps because she grew up in an orphanage in Syracuse, New York. In those days, men were discouraged from raising children alone, and Grandpa Sam had no choice but to put her there after his first wife, her mother, died. She never talked of it, even when I would ask questions, but I'm certain it affected her. Regardless, I knew never to cross her, and her guilt trips were worse than any spanking.

Growing up, my mother was admired in the Jewish community. She worked on all the committees and was involved in planning and producing many Jewish events. She never learned to drive a car, and ran all her errands and attended all her meetings by taking the bus. She learned to transfer from bus to bus to get to her destinations. Her stamina and energy were boundless and I am grateful that I inherited this from her.

Bedonna was born three years after me. She was always the pretty one, with dark black, curly hair, while my blonde hair was straight. When we were young, we fought all the time and she always won. I was a prissy sissy compared to her. So as we grew, I began to realize that our interests would polarize. In fact, we were total opposites; she was the tomboy, I was the bookworm. She would climb trees; I'd paint pictures. She was Mommy's girl; I was Daddy's girl.

Even today, while Bedonna and I have a loving sister relationship, we are still totally opposite. She embraces the Jewish faith and her family observes and lives within Jewish culture. Bedonna thinks nothing of getting on a Harley Davidson motorcycle, skiing, or kayaking, while I prefer an air-conditioned luxury tour bus or sunbathing on a pristine beach. Bedonna lives at a quiet ski resort and loves the remote country atmosphere, while I prefer to live near a big city with all the busy activities associated there.

I have vivid memories of climbing up into Daddy's lap and asking, "Daddy, don't you wish you had a boy?" Daddy would smile and brush my hair from my eyes and say, "No, my little *Sheyne Meydele*, I always wanted two girls; one blonde named Gerrie and one brunette called Bedonna." I'd kiss his cute bald spot, then jump down to go and play, comforted in that assurance that I was treasured and loved.

As I grew, I was drawn to any and every fine art activity I could try. I dabbled in dance, then moved on to visual arts, and also tried my luck with theatre. Creativity and culture were my forte, so naturally I grew to love reading. In fact, it was my favorite thing to do. Knowing my love for books, Mother walked me to the library twice every week, which seemed like countless blocks from our house. But they were worth the walk because books opened new worlds for me. They held a special fragrance and I inhaled their aromas deeply each time we entered the library. I became an avid reader. Mother had high hopes for me, and she and Daddy desired that I be successful in whatever I did. I was their child; they knew I had the capabilities, so success was anticipated.

Chapter 2

GROWING UP JEWISH

ROWING UP, I loved being a member of the Jewish community. But I confess, I didn't apply myself at Hebrew school. In fact, I flunked! It was so boring to me. When we went to the synagogue on Friday nights, I sat in the back and passed notes with whoever was sitting next to me. After services we would eat rugelach and dance our folk dances. Despite how much I loved the Jewish traditions each week, there was still something missing. I didn't know God. For me, being Jewish was more a culture than a religion. The religious part just seemed like a bunch of rules.

I used to sneak out of services during the high holidays as we were in school all day. I would hang out with my friends at the drug store for a quick Coke, breaking the fast that was practiced on Yom Kippur in our conservative congregation.

One of the traditions of the high holy holidays was a complete new outfit. I loved showing off my new dress, jewelry, and shoes to my friends, and I loved seeing their new styles as well. Simply, I just loved being with "my people." There was always laughter. Jewish people are the only ones I know who can be talking all at the same time and yet everyone knows what the other is saying.

Holidays were always our favorite. I can remember as a

child wanting to have Christmas like other kids because the Christmas trees were so pretty. Even though we had Hanukah, which lasted eight days, I still wanted a Christmas tree. One day walking home from school, just shortly after Christmas, when people had already discarded their Christmas trees, I discovered a small discarded tree near a trashcan. I hauled the pitiful little thing home and hid it under my bed not thinking my mother would find it. Mother of course discovered it and when she asked me what it was doing there, I told her it was a Hanukah bush!

Our family would go to Chicago in the summers and live with my grandparents in one of the Jewish neighborhoods. All the kids would gather on a street corner on that North side of Chicago and laugh and play the evenings away. We would meet in front of the butcher shop on the corner. The grocery store next door that had the best kosher dill pickles in their barrel. Grandpa used to give us money to go pick out our pickles. Next to that was a candy store and the synagogue was next to that. It was a classic Jewish neighborhood, and Bedonna and I looked forward to visiting each summer.

The only bad memory of those summers was the noise on Friday mornings. My bedroom window was just across the street from the butcher shop. Each Friday morning I would awaken to the sounds of chickens being killed for the Sabbath meal. I always wondered later in that evening if I was eating one of the squawkers. I remember that Grandma (Grandpa Sam's second wife) would spend all day on Friday to prepare the Shabbat.

I can still remember when we called other kids to come and play we yelled, "Yo! Phyllis!" I remember riding the streetcars with Mother when she would take us to see the celebrities who were appearing in the downtown theatre. It was a big part of Mother's life, so it became ours, too. My father's sister, Aunt Clara, would always tell me, "Geraldine, when you grow up and get married, you can fall in love with a rich man just as easily as a poor man."

As I grew up and starting thinking about dating, it was important to my family that I dated Jewish boys. I was strongly discouraged from dating outside of my faith. I enjoyed the Jewish boys that I dated. My first love was a nice Jewish boy in the neighborhood who treated me well. He was, by far, the cutest boy in the synagogue and the best dancer in school, as well. But I soon lost interest in dating the boys I grew up with.

One summer in Chicago I thought I fell in love with another handsome, yet typical Jewish boy. He had dark curly hair. He was such a smooth dancer that he stole my heart. Nothing ever became of that relationship, either. Although I had fun with them, I never found what I was looking for in those boys.

As I grew up, I began to search for a deeper meaning to being Jewish. I thought that if I went to school on Friday nights it would make me more religious. But even when I tried my hardest to pay attention and glean something from those services, I never felt anything spiritual, one way or another. It wasn't uncommon for people to have loud conversations during the service, but I'm sure I overdid it!

I loved those times when I could hang out with my favorite relative, my cousin Larry Rose. He was three years older than me and was my best friend. We fought like brother and sister, but bonded from the cradle. We were best friends through high school and college. When I married Clyde, Larry never said how disappointed he was, but I knew just the same. Despite this, Larry and I remain as close as ever.

Chapter 3

THE FIRST TIME
I PRAYED

IREMEMBER PRAYING FOR the first time when I was about sixteen. I was beginning to have doubts about God. I knew there was a supreme Being, but growing up in a Jewish home, following Jewish traditions, didn't mean that I was taught to think of God as Someone with whom I could have a relationship.

I wandered into the synagogue in Chicago, across the street from my grandmother's house, searching for something that would satisfy my emptiness. The night was warm and sultry and filled with the big city smells of rye bread and garlic, mixed with diesel fumes from the street. It was the first time I could remember praying. It was there that God began to reveal Himself and to call me. It was there that I asked Him to show me what was right.

At that point in my life, I believed in God but He didn't seem real to me. He wasn't tangible and certainly wasn't near. He was a vague Notion, not a Presence, and while I wanted to find something or someone grounded to my Jewish roots, He just seemed so far away. There in the synagogue, on that warm summer evening, I discovered that I had a deep longing to have a relationship with God.

I left the synagogue confused and sad. I had discovered that I wanted a relationship with God, but I did not find one there. I did not even find anything there that might have showed me how to search for one.

Chapter 4

OY VEY—COURTING TROUBLE

As WORLD WAR II ended, being Jewish wasn't quite as difficult. It was easier to blend in with the other students. At Kalamazoo Central High School, I had a lot of friends and I was always the social butterfly. I had many Gentile friends, but dating was still a Jewish-boys-only situation.

It became clear to my parents that they may have spoiled me a bit too much, and when I was fifteen Daddy decided I should learn responsibility through working. I got my first job at Steinberg's Deli. Although Mr. Steinberg was a friend of my father's, he didn't put up with me for very long. Mr. Steinberg was quite frugal, and behind the scenes he sailed a very tight ship. He cut corners in many ways, and on my first day he had me water down the ketchups.

I couldn't remember how much water he told me to put in so I just walked up to him and asked, "How much water would you like me to put in the ketchup, Mr. Steinberg?" I wasn't aware I shouldn't have done that in front of the customers, but it was visibly apparent that he was upset. At the end of the day Mr. Steinberg paid me my first and final paycheck. *Oy Vey!*

~

When I was sixteen, the time came to get my driver's license. We had a big navy-blue Hudson car. It was a huge sedan and hard for me to handle. I wasn't quite five-feet-tall, and could barely see up over the steering wheel. Daddy took me down to take my driver's test and I flunked it. There was no doubt that I was not qualified to drive on the roads of Michigan. But Daddy and the tester had a little talk—I can't say that money was exchanged, but it must have been—after which I was granted my Michigan driver's license anyway!

Daddy and I went to Holly's Restaurant to celebrate. In Holly's parking lot there was a big round sign on a pole that read, "Holly's parking." I crashed our Hudson right into the sign! The sign was dented and so was Daddy's beautiful car. I never wanted to drive again, but Daddy just paid for the damages and made me drive home.

It was during this time in my life when the dynamics between my mother and me began to change. I was starting to seek relief from the constant bickering, though it wasn't entirely my mother's fault. I never felt that I had measured up to her expectations, an opinion that would hold true in later years as well.

I sought comfort with my favorite aunt, my cousin Larry's mother, Aunt Rose Rose. (Yes, her first and last names were Rose—*and* she lived on Rose Street, no less.) Aunt Rose was my father's sister and had the same disposition. When mother was so difficult, I would go to my Aunt Rose for advice, because she was sympathetic, understanding, and always made me feel loved.

I was too young emotionally when I graduated from high school at age seventeen, but when conflicts with my mother became stressful my relatives in Detroit offered to have me come stay with them. I eagerly accepted. They fixed up a beautiful apartment for me and welcomed me with warmth and typical Jewish hospitality. I really felt mature in that apartment; I felt like a "big city girl" that had finally arrived. I stayed a few months, working at the telephone company. Before long, Mother insisted I come back home. I finally agreed because I missed Daddy, and strangely enough I missed my mother, too. I also realized that I hadn't found what I was looking for in my new independence.

Chapter 5

At the Cross-Roads

OON AFTER I arrived home, it didn't take long for
me to find my friends and enjoy my previous social
life. My security was in having people like me, in
going to parties and receiving compliments. I could hardly
wait to get back into the social scene. On one occasion, my
closest girlfriend, Eileen, who was Catholic, had a date with
a young man named Clyde, whom she thought was "Mr.
Wonderful." Eileen was making social plans and needed
somebody to go out with a friend of "Mr. Wonderful."
I agreed to help her out.

Well, this Clyde was anything but wonderful to me. Oh
he was tall, very handsome in a John Wayne sort of way. He
had a confident swagger, quick wit, and piercing brown eyes.
But he was not wonderful in my opinion; in fact, I thought
he was very rude.

Back in those days, I smoked with a rhinestone-studded
cigarette holder, and was rather confident in myself. I don't
mean to brag, but I didn't have to work very hard to get a
young man's attention. Yet, when Clyde passed out popcorn
that night he passed me up! I said to myself, "How distasteful!"
and I felt embarrassed at the slight from Clyde in front of
the group of friends. I grew up with a fondness for sparkle,

jewels, and glamour for the attention they drew. I resented Clyde's actions.

But I put up with Clyde because he was Eileen's boyfriend, and they would often ask me to accompany them on outings or dates as a third party, if I wasn't busy. I would always consent to them, for it was better than staying home. In fact, we started enjoying the three party evenings, and slowly I began to see another side to Clyde and he began to see another side of me.

It didn't take long for an attraction to blossom between Eileen's "Mr. Wonderful" and me. Clyde no longer seemed rude and obnoxious, but instead I thought he was adorable! One night, Clyde called to ask me for advice on how to talk to Eileen about the religious differences between them. Clyde was Protestant and there were too many conflicts between Eileen's Catholic beliefs and his. I had my eye on Clyde, and I couldn't help but wonder how opposite I would be with my Jewish background, compared to that?

Clyde and I had our first date as an informal meeting over a Coke to talk about the concerns he felt about Eileen's faith. I detected that this was just an excuse for the two of us to be together. It seemed to me that Clyde really liked me and I recognized a sweetness revealed by the two of us being together. We looked into each others' eyes, but we didn't dare divulge our inner thoughts for one another.

Eileen was my best friend. My conscience would ask, "How can you do this to her?" But Clyde had such a charm about him, and he was so refreshingly different from anyone I'd ever known or dated before. I'd dated a few Gentiles, and I loved how much Clyde cared for his five sisters and how he adored his mother.

Clyde was three years older than me and had returned from a tour in the Navy. He was mature, self-assured, and so handsome with those big brown eyes, thick wavy hair, and confident smile. There was a sweetness about him, too, that complimented his quick wit. When I was with Clyde we laughed a lot and he had the most impeccable manners. I was captivated by his charm and good looks.

Several times, as we shared Cokes, I listened to Clyde's concerns about what kind of future he and Eileen could have with their vast religious differences. Catholics and Protestants were strongly discouraged from marrying in those days. I found myself anxiously awaiting our Coke counsel.

One time, Clyde asked me for a date to have pizza. The closest pizza place was more than fifty miles away, so I told him if he got there on time, I would buy the pizza. Clyde's strategy was well planned for this option. He arrived early at my home and sat out front until one minute before the time he was scheduled to arrive. That was the last time I ever paid for anything from then until now!

That began the clandestine courtship between Clyde and me. Clyde didn't kiss me on the first date, but after that first kiss, I was hooked. Of course both sets of parents were totally unaware of the love budding between us. Clyde and I kept our new relationship undercover for a few weeks.

Clyde's family owned a recreation area known as Big Lake. We loved to drive out there and sit by the lake and talk. It was about a month after we started secretly dating that Clyde drove to the top of the hill overlooking Big Lake and stopped the car. The radio was playing softly as we looked over the blue water. Clyde gathered me into his arms, kissed me tenderly, and told me that he loved me. My heart was racing and I gasped a quick breath before I told him that I loved him, too, as The Four Aces sang "Three Coins in the Fountain" in the background.

~

Eventually, I told my parents that I had a strong attraction for Clyde. There was no discussion between us—just screaming, ranting, and raving that I would not date a Gentile. It was not a topic for discussion. Their word was law, and they would not consider any dialogue regarding Clyde. They expected that I would honor this demand without question, for they could only remember I had never been a disobedient daughter and that I had always complied with all their requests. They simply forbade me to see Clyde again. And to insure that I would follow their orders, they insisted I go to Chicago on weekends to date the Jewish boys there.

Their plan was simple. Each Friday they took me to the train station to send me to Chicago. And they were waiting for me, at the same train station, to come back in on Sunday night. I was under the watchful eye of my Jewish relatives the entire weekend; this seemed to Mother and Daddy like a foolproof plan to find me a "nice Jewish boy" to marry.

What they didn't know was that Clyde parked his brand new green 1953 Ford parallel to the train tracks, a few blocks down from the station. He would leave Kalamazoo in his car at the same time my train pulled out of the station. He drove part of the way to Chicago alongside the train tracks. I would sit in my seat at the window and blow kisses to him. After a few weeks, some of the other regular train passengers would wave to him with me.

Clyde had family who lived in Chicago, so he would stay in the Windy City each weekend, too. He met me at the

Chicago train station, and we arranged the charade that he was my taxi cab driver who would take me to my grandparent's house in Chicago. I would get out of his car about a block before we got to my grandparent's house and get in the backseat. When we arrived at my grandparent's house, I would get out of the car and even pretend to tip him! On Sunday night, when I called the taxi to return to take me to the train station, it would be Clyde in his same green Ford. My grandparents were too elderly and unsuspecting to know what was going on. This sham worked well for Clyde and me.

Spending time with Clyde had to be carefully choreographed each week. I had to go out with the Jewish boys in Chicago all weekend, but Clyde and I would talk on the telephone in between dates. And the time we did spend together in secret meeting places was priceless.

On one of the weekends in Chicago I went to a nightclub with a fellow. Looking back, I can see that it was a time that God really worked in my life, even though I was unaware of it.

I loved getting all dressed up, feeling like I looked pretty, going to the parties and receiving compliments. I reveled in the trappings of being young and able to capture the attention of my friends. But no matter how special the event, how stunning the dress, or how striking the jewelry, when it was all over I would feel completely empty.

This wasn't a one-time incident, either; it was time and time again. On one of those occasions, my date took me to the Blue Note nightclub in Chicago where Debbie Reynolds was appearing. It was a glamorous night, filled with the magic of Debbie's talent. Everyone seemed to be captivated by the show, but I felt distracted. I remember looking across the crowd as she sang. I looked in the eyes of the other club patrons around me and wondered if they felt as empty as I did. They all had smiles, but so did I. It almost seemed like their smiles were plastic, as if there were painted on for show.

I had known there was something lacking in my life before this, but that moment at the Blue Note clearly defined it for me. When I got home, as I undid the clasp on my necklace and got out of my beautiful gown, a sudden sadness surrounded my heart and an unexplainable heaviness gripped me in wonder—was this it? Would I just exist from party to party all my life?

The shallowness of my life surfaced and I longed for comfort or assurance that my life had purpose. I got into bed and listened to the familiar sounds of the night. I could hear the delivery trucks, horses whinnying, and cars backfiring. I could hear footsteps coming up the walk and tried to distinguish who was coming home by the sounds. Early in the morning, I was still lying there, listening as I heard the iceman delivering large blocks of ice for our refrigerator. I knew there would be melted ice drips along the stairs about now. I heard squeaking hinges, doors opening and slamming, and heavy boots on the stairway.

Pulling the blanket over my head, I tried to drown out the sounds and sadness, but I knew I would need to wait until the iceman had made a few more stops. I pulled the blanket up tighter around me, burrowing into the covers. Yet the darkness of the night's revelation still shrouded my heart.

Chapter 6

CLANDESTINE IN CHICAGO

C LYDE AND I continued our covert Chicago meetings. One week, as we were making our plans for
our Chicago taxi weekends, I decided to take the
chance of riding most of the way home from Chicago in
the car with Clyde. He wasn't so sure this was a good idea.
"Gerrie," he cautioned me in his deep voice, "are you sure?
It's a bit of a risk."

"Oh Clyde!" I laughed, "just think, we can enjoy the whole
trip back. It will be such fun."

We plotted that Clyde would pick me up at my grandmother's house as usual, posing as the taxi driver. I'd get in
the back seat, and then move to the front as soon as we were
out of Grandmother's neighborhood. We'd skip the Chicago
train station and I would simply get on the train at the Niles
station, the stop before my final destination in Kalamazoo.

This meant that Clyde and I would be able to spend more
than two hours together in his car for the return trip. I could
snuggle next to him and we would be encapsulated in the
car, without anyone telling us that our relationship was
forbidden.

The plan seemed flawless and extremely exciting. I placed a pretend phone call for a taxi, and shortly thereafter, Clyde drove up. He put my suitcase into the trunk, opened the back door of the car for me, and I got in. My taxi driver drove me off to the train station as I waved to my grandparents. A few blocks down the street, Clyde pulled over and I got out of the backseat and into the front seat of his car.

We were thrilled to be together for a road trip. This time I wouldn't be blowing kisses out the window of the train, but instead, I'd be snuggled right next to Clyde for 150 glorious miles! We started for home in that new Ford, with Clyde's right arm around me, and I cuddled up next to him. It was such a great feeling to be together and so in love.

About fifty miles north of Chicago, we ran into a violent midwestern thunderstorm. The clouds went from gray to dark blue to almost black as vicious winds snapped tree branches and debris danced dramatically across the road in front of us. The rain poured down horizontally, and Clyde slowed the car, tense with what was developing. We had to arrive at Niles station on time, or I was going to have a lot of explaining to do.

The winds increased and thunder roared as lightning splintered the sky around us. When the hail began to pound on the hood and roof of Clyde's car with golf-ball size stones, Clyde had to pull over. It was a Micah hailstorm with tornado-force winds, and it was impossible to continue on. Clyde stopped the car and I knew that I would miss my train in Niles.

Mother and Daddy met the train in Kalamazoo at the regularly scheduled time. When I did not get off the train they were extremely alarmed. They called my grandmother in Chicago to confirm that I had gotten on the train to come home.

My mother was fearful and asked my grandmother, "Did Gerrie get off all right? She wasn't on the train."

Grandmother replied, "Yes, Sadie, I saw her take the taxi."

Before my mother could ask another question, my grandmother told her, in a thick Yiddish accent, "But Sadie, I don't know who that taxi cab driver is, but she's in love with him."

Mother's reaction was, "Oy, Vey! I know who it is!" There had been battles between my family and I before, but this began the war.

When the thunderstorm had subsided, Clyde drove me home. There was no use trying to continue the charade of the train station any longer. When we arrived at my house, Clyde dropped me off and I went into the house by myself. The tirade began.

"How could you do this to us? What were you thinking? He is not a Jew!" Crying, screaming, threats, insults; they flew around the room in heated turmoil. Mother and Daddy wouldn't listen to me and they blamed everything about our forbidden relationship on Clyde.

Later that night, Clyde knocked on the door. I let him in, but when he entered the foyer, both my mother and father refused to welcome him into our home. That traditional warm, loving, Jewish welcome was replaced with hostility and glares, and then in no uncertain terms both my mother and father told Clyde never to enter their doorstep again. They instructed him not to talk to me, not to see me, and there was to be no contact, anywhere! Clyde was given strict orders that he was never allowed back on the premises.

"Things are going to change," my mother warned me as Clyde stood there, stunned at the tirade, "and they're going to change in a hurry."

I was screaming hysterically, begging them to understand how much I cared for Clyde. Mother and Daddy wouldn't listen to me. As far as they were concerned, this was all Clyde's fault and it was a closed subject. I was their daughter; I would do what was ordered. I would not see Clyde again, period.

Chapter 7

A Turning Point

I WAS DEVASTATED. I didn't have anyone to comfort me. I didn't know how to go to God for comfort. Clyde had been ordered out the door and out of my life. And when it closed, my mother turned to me and shrieked, "When I get my hands on you, there'll be nothing left!"

Distraught and fearful, I ran out the door, down the street in our quiet, subdued, respectable neighborhood, with my mother screaming after me, my father shouting and running after her, and my sister crying and running after the two of them. I ran to my aunt's house, about three blocks up the hill, thinking she would protect me from Mother.

But when I arrived at her house, I found out differently; she grabbed me and pulled me in with Mother, Daddy, and Bedonna soon to follow. It turned out that everyone in my extended family was determined to end my relationship with Clyde.

Clyde and I agreed to honor my parents' wishes. It broke my heart, but it seemed so impossible for us to ever have a relationship with all their protest. Clyde and I stopped seeing each other, and I no longer looked forward to his phone calls. But our love was not that easily squelched. My heart ached to see Clyde and I missed him desperately. He was always on my mind and there was a hole in my heart where he belonged.

One day, I was driving down Highway 37 north of Kalamazoo. I kept thinking of Clyde and wondering where he was, and what he was doing. I smiled as I thought of how much I loved him, and wiped a tear from my cheek as I thought of the love we had lost. It was almost like a mirage when I noticed, in the oncoming traffic ahead, Clyde's green Ford.

I slammed on the brakes and pulled my car to the side of the road. About that time, Clyde recognized my car, and he pulled over to the other side of the road. We ran to the middle of the highway into a desperate embrace as cars whipped past us from both directions. Standing in the traffic, Clyde whispered in my ear as he held me tight, "Gerrie, I know how much you love me, and I know how much I love you. We cannot remain apart. Our love can get us through this—whatever it takes."

The next weeks and months were tumultuous. I would talk with Clyde by phone, and Eileen, who had forgiven me for stealing him from her, agreed to help us. She set up meetings and passed along messages. We would meet at her house, where we could sit and talk.

One day Clyde and I met in front of Eileen's house. He parked along the curb and I got in his car, so happy to be spending time with him. About that time, my father drove up and there Clyde and I were in the car.

Daddy was beside himself. He didn't know what to do to convince me of the folly in dating a Gentile. He and mother decided that they would lock me in my room until I came to my senses. I was almost nineteen-years-old! It didn't matter to them. I was their daughter and I needed their guidance.

I stayed exiled in my room as told, but I refused to eat for three days. A Jewish mother can't bear to have her child miss a meal. I knew this was playing "dirty" against my mother, but it was my only ammunition. I was desperate to see Clyde, and my mother was desperate to get me to abide by her wishes. She didn't want me to starve, but in her mind, that would have been better than me running around with Clyde. Mother tried everything to settle me down and listen to reason, pleading with me to eat something. I finally caved in and agreed to eat on the fourth day, when I smelled the aroma of her chicken soup.

One night I had a glimmer of hope. Mother was off attending a committee meeting when Daddy came into my room and allowed me to see Clyde. "Make your peace, Gerrie. He's not a Jew; he's not a good mate for you." Daddy didn't say it, but this action showed me that he recognized many of the qualities I admired in Clyde. "Be back within the hour," Daddy warned me, "way before your mother returns."

Mother and Daddy finally stated some terms that would allow me to see Clyde. They proposed that if Clyde would convert to Judaism, and if we didn't see each other for a year, that if after a year we still felt the same way about one another, they would reconsider our relationship. Mother and Daddy were certain that this was a passing infatuation. They were convinced that if Clyde and I simply didn't see each other for a while, it would pass.

That same day I was allowed to see Clyde to explain their terms. Clyde wasn't welcome in our home, but I could talk with him in the car, parked in front of the house. The contract my parents had proposed wasn't agreeable to me or to Clyde, but it at least gave me an opportunity to see him. I was so desperate I was willing to go along with their terms. After what we'd been going through, all their conditions seemed almost reasonable to me.

Sitting there in that car, Clyde gave me a letter that his mother had written to him. Carefully, I unfolded the paper and read his mother's fluid handwriting, "Clyde, if you love this Jewish girl as much as you say you do, it seems to your father and me that you would want her to live for eternity, not just a short time here on earth."

I refolded the paper and handed it back to Clyde, stunned. I felt very judged at that point. Clyde's parents didn't even know me. How could they know where I would spend eternity?

I was totally unaware of what Clyde's mother was referring to, or what the Bible said about eternal life. I had not even met Clyde's parents.

My reaction was that I wanted Clyde to talk to the Rabbi. Clyde agreed, but he wanted me to talk to a minister to know what he believed.

That was fair. So we decided to go to the minister first. I insisted that the minister had to be in a town several miles away where no one would know me. My parents were well known in Kalamazoo. It was imperative that Mother and Daddy not find out that I was even listening to Christian counsel.

It was a daring move for me to open my mind to listen to Christian teachings. I was fearful and deeply rooted in my Jewish heritage, only doing this to please Clyde. Yet, God knew where to lead me. I really didn't know many Protestant people at that time.

I was very uncomfortable going into the minister's home, despite it being a pleasant white frame house, trimmed in gray with a welcoming front porch. There were dahlias blooming, cheerfully waving to us in the wind with their bright yellows and purples as I walked up to the door. Warmly we were welcomed in. Clyde and I sat on a sofa with a flowered pattern, and I remember the window shades being pulled half way down. I was so nervous, I didn't know what to expect, but I didn't think it would be good.

~

BIG DECISIONS

At first it was awkward and uncomfortable, but after being there just a short time, my fears disintegrated. The minister was kind and friendly, and he welcomed me with warmth reminiscent of Jewish traditions. We started talking at 8:30 in the morning and continued throughout the entire day.

It was clear that we had different reasons for talking. I wanted to talk to him about getting married to this man I loved; he wanted to talk about the Bible.

He asked me if I ever read the Bible. I told him no, and that even though I had glanced through it a time or two, it meant nothing to me. I was not even allowed to read the New Testament of the Bible, so that was completely foreign to me.

The minister asked me, "Gerrie, have you ever known anybody who had sinned?"

It caught me off guard. "No," I replied. "I know about Hitler and Eichmann," assuming that's what sin was, and that was what he was referring to as well.

This kind, patient man went on to explain that telling a lie was sin. Oops! I thought how I had lied to my family about where I was going that morning. Then the minister informed me that cheating was a sin. Oops! I thought about how I had done my share of cheating in class, and I knew most of the others had, too.

He went on with more examples of sin and I found myself guilty of many sins. It was the first time I'd thought of sin as more than just things like the horrible drama of Hitler, notorious bank robbers, or heartless murders. Sin was me.

Even though I was considered a "good girl," he taught me that I had sinned. I had sinned in many ways. As Jews, we read everything from the Old Testament. This minister introduced me to new holy words from the New Testament that stirred in my heart.

First, he asked if it would be all right to show me some verses in the New Testament. I agreed. He compared verses from the Old Testament such as Psalm 22:1, "My God, my God, why have you abandoned me?" with Matthew 27:46.

I was interested, but still confused. Even though he shared many verses to show me that Jesus was the Messiah, I really didn't understand what he was saying. It was so unfamiliar. As a Jew, I knew about the promised Messiah, but I wasn't seeking Him. What I wanted for my life was a peace and the fulfillment of the emptiness I felt. I wanted to know God in a more personal way. I just didn't think it was possible.

Then he came to the verse I really understood—John 3:16, "For God loved the world so much that he gave his one and only Son, so that everyone who believes in him will not perish but have eternal life." After he repeated the verse, he had me repeat it. He could see that I was beginning to have an understanding.

Then he said, "Let's put your name in instead of 'the world'."

So I read out loud, "For God so loved Gerrie, that he gave his only son, that if Gerrie would believe in Him, Gerrie would not perish, but Gerrie would have everlasting life."

It was the first time I really thought about everlasting life. What a curious thought; living forever with God. Why, that was unimaginable! I was enjoying the moment, yet as we were talking, I kept thinking of what my parents would say if they knew where I was.

Something compelled me to keep going. I know now it was God. But then, I just knew it was something I desired. I had this deep hunger to know God and the anticipation that I might actually find Him here.

And then I remembered. It came to the forefront of my mind, the time I went to the synagogue praying that I would know what was right. I remembered my time at the Blue Note Club, wondering if those people felt as empty as I did. It was as if pieces to a heavenly puzzle were softly floating about the room, falling together to make a clear picture. I was excited and invigorated, trying to figure everything out.

The minister made it very clear that in order to have peace and fulfillment, it would be through Jesus Christ. And the only way I would have heaven assured would be through Jesus Christ.

In my heart I knew he was right. I was in awe because this minister was the first person who really had answers for all my questions. And that day I had hundreds of questions.

Late that afternoon we thanked him for all the time he'd spent with us. As we gathered our things to leave, the minister said, "Well, Gerrie, you are at a crossroad. You know the truth that God requires to have eternal life, and it's up to you to make that decision of which road you want to take."

I started to cry. Gently he continued to explain to me that in order to have this relationship that I desired, I needed to tell God I was sorry for my sin, and to ask Jesus Christ to come into my life.

This was more than I could do. You see, I wanted to pray for *God* to come into my life, *not Jesus*. My innermost longing was to know God, not to know Jesus. I didn't understand who Jesus was, or how He was associated with God. As a Jew, I was afraid to say the name of Jesus. So I walked out of the house and toward the car.

I began to cry again. I was trying so hard not to, yet the tears came anyway. It was God working in my life, softening my heart as He called me. I wanted to get out of there, but I was afraid to leave in fear that I would never find anybody again who knew the answers regarding the longing in my heart.

Those who knew me back then thought I didn't have any longings. I had plenty of friends, a nice family, everything that most people would have loved to have. But what no one knew was that my friends were my security and all the parties kept my mind occupied. I was busy and having fun, but it was all so empty. I was so young and to me the future didn't look enticing. I kept wondering if superficial things were all my life was going to consist of. I just thought that was the way it had to be for everybody.

Now here I was, with this man telling me that I could have a personal relationship with God through Jesus.

I remember standing by Clyde's green Ford. I looked at the minister, and taking a ragged breath I changed my mind, "I think I'd like to pray with you," I said.

In my heart I knew I was going to pray, but inside I vowed that I would never tell anybody. This would be a little secret between God and me. I didn't want the repercussions of what that would do within my family.

Clyde, the minister, and I went back in the house, where the minister suggested that we get on our knees to pray. I had never prayed to Jesus, let alone get on my knees to pray! But I nodded in agreement. We got on our knees and he told me to repeat a prayer after him, "Dear Jesus, I'm asking You to come into my heart and life and save me," I said in a timid voice. "I know You died for me. Forgive me for all I've done wrong."

It was the prayer of a little child, and I couldn't pray it. I couldn't say that name of Jesus. Somehow, I knew that what he said was true, yet I just couldn't say it. We stopped and he informed me that Jesus was God, and the only way to God would be through Jesus Christ.

I thought, "Okay, I can do this. I'm going to pray this prayer, and not tell a soul!"

I should have known better, for when a Jewish girl finds such a deal, she can't keep it to herself.

We prayed and I in child-like faith asked Jesus to come into my heart. I didn't expect anything to happen. Instead, my heart was overcome with happiness, relief, and a new joy; I experienced the happiest emotion I'd ever felt in my life. I never doubted Jesus again in my lifetime, even though I've disappointed Him many times.

It surprised me because suddenly I didn't know which was love for God and which was love for Clyde. This time I thanked the minister for his time with my new heart.

As we began the ride home, we talked about our future. Clyde was a professing Christian, and he knew he wanted a Christian wife. We drove toward home, deliriously happy, and decided between the two of us that we were no longer "unequally yoked" (KJV) a term used in 2 Corinthians 6:14 that warns couples of conflicting faiths from marrying. That was what we had heard from both his parents and mine— that our future together was doomed to failure because we were of two different faiths.

Now we found ourselves of the same faith, both of us accepting Jesus as our Savior. So it seemed perfectly reasonable and appropriate for us to make permanent life plans. We decided to elope.

We picked up two friends along the way, and stopped at Clyde's parents' house to inform them of what we were going to do. They were so thankful to hear that I had become a new Christian, they didn't want to discourage the marriage.

We drove to Angola, Indiana, where you could be married in four hours. We found a little chapel in a garden with a trellis full of pink and white roses, purple lilacs, and lots of greenery framing the doorway. It was a tiny chapel that held only six people. There we exchanged wedding vows, promising to love each other until death. This was a far cry from the traditional Jewish wedding rituals of the Chuppa, or the breaking of the wine glass, my parents had dreamed of for me.

Once I was married, I knew that I had to tell Mother and Daddy and I knew it wouldn't be pleasant. So rather than call them, I sent them a telegram saying, "Clyde and I were joined in holy matrimony this morning. Sorry you don't understand. Love, Gerrie."

Chapter 8

OUR FIRST NIGHT

OUR WEDDING NIGHT was the first time Clyde and I were ever intimate. On this first night to sleep together, I was too afraid to let Clyde see me in my pretty nightie. I didn't want to come out of the bathroom. Clyde was very patient, and assured me that it would be all right. So I wrapped myself in his red plaid, flannel shirt.

"I'm not coming out unless you turn out the lights," I told him.

"All right, Gerrie," Clyde agreed. "Whatever you say."

I peeked out the bathroom door and sure enough, the room was dark. Clyde had turned out the light.

"Promise not to turn the lights back on?" I asked, suspiciously.

"Of course," Clyde confirmed.

Timidly, I stepped out of the bathroom, when Clyde flipped the light switch back on. I squealed and dashed beneath the covers of the bed. As passionately as I felt about Clyde, becoming a wife was a bold new adventure I wasn't quite sure of.

That first morning in our little apartment, Clyde woke up looking for breakfast.

"Hey, Honey," Clyde grinned. "Why don't you make me some breakfast?"

I was stunned. Me? Cook breakfast? I didn't know how to boil water or cook an egg.

"What do you mean?" I inquired innocently. "I don't cook."

Clyde sighed. "There are eggs in the refrigerator."

"I don't know how to cook eggs," I told him truthfully. "I don't cook. I've never cooked, and I don't care if I ever learn to cook."

Clyde didn't believe me. "How could anybody not know how to cook an egg? It's not that difficult," Clyde coaxed. "In fact, it will be fun."

I wasn't buying this deal at all. "We don't have a frying pan."

"We have a pan and we have water. We can boil the eggs." Clyde explained.

I'd never boiled water. "I don't know how to boil water," I admitted to Clyde.

This began my culinary education. Clyde thought I was exaggerating and couldn't imagine that I didn't have any kitchen skills. He learned a lot after that day. The truth was I knew nothing about anything.

When we first moved into our little apartment Clyde had rented, I decided not to let Mother and Daddy know where we were. But Mother and Daddy contacted our friends and told our friends to find us.

Mother and Daddy were desperate to remove me from this marriage. They wouldn't come to our little home, but instead arranged a meeting at their house where they offered Clyde "whatever it took" (meaning money) to annul the marriage.

Mother and Daddy assured him that they could make the arrangements.

It was tense, angry, volatile, and there were many tears. It was clear that Mother and Daddy were not going to accept Clyde as my husband. They were shocked that I would run away and disobey, and they demanded that I come home. It was a terrible, terrible day with Clyde and me refusing to adhere to their demands. I was exhausted when we left. Sobbing in the car I thought about how as a child the Gentiles had hurt me in countless ways because I was Jewish; and now, my own people were hurting me far more deeply.

The next day I got a phone call that my father was in the hospital. I rushed to the hospital to hear my mother admonish me, screaming at the top of her lungs, "Look what you've done to your father!" as she waved her arms toward the hospital bed. "Are you satisfied? Is this what you want for your father?" she demanded. "Now he's had a heart attack!"

I was beyond devastated. I loved Daddy. Had I really done this to him? Had my disobedience to his will caused a heart attack? Grief and guilt swarmed around me with large looming clouds of despair. But again God intervened. The family doctor we'd had all our lives entered the room and examined Daddy. Then he talked to mother. Finally, he wanted to talk to Clyde and me.

Walking down the hospital corridor, he put his arm around each of us and said, "Gerrie, your father has not had a heart attack, he has a broken heart. And he'll be better in a few days."

I felt such relief. And I held fast to my love for Clyde and my newfound Christian faith.

For weeks I was admonished, scolded, and chastised by every aunt, uncle, cousin, and family friend I knew. My Aunt Clara grabbed my arm in her anger and clawed me as she tried to make her point. Even though Mother agreed with Aunt Clara, she was very upset when she saw the blood on my arm. Yet, to the entire family, it was somehow justified, because it was beyond belief that I would dishonor my family by chasing after a Gentile boy. Collectively my family was determined to bring me to my senses.

The only time my Aunt Clara ever spoke to me for years afterward was if my father or mother were present. Beyond that, she completely ignored me. The marriage was a shock to the Jewish community and they tried to figure out what to do to make sense of it. Some of the family sat together and they mourned that I had done such a foolish, disgraceful thing. I was unable to comfort them, and I just cried.

Aunt Rose was the one person that I knew would understand my love for Clyde and that I had no choice but to run away. She immediately started gathering things for our little apartment and ignored the anger of all my other relatives. It made me realize the importance of always having an understanding heart for others who are in need.

Aunt Rose was my one comfort. She was there every day that I needed her. Jewish tradition dictated that I should have a lavish bridal shower and the aunts were in charge. While Aunt Rose organized, even Aunt Clara had to be part of it.

Amazingly, even though the family did not approve of the marriage, all my aunts helped plan, prepare, and pay for a beautiful, extravagant party at a hotel. All the family came with generous gifts of silver and china, for me to start my married life with Clyde. Later I realized that they didn't do any of it for me, they did it to comfort my mother.

Yet not all memories of that time are sad. My new faith was exciting. I had not been a strong-willed child, but my new faith was so real that I had confidence to stand up to Mother and Daddy. I knew that what I'd found was real. I didn't know how to grow in it yet, but I knew it had made a difference. That's when I became closer and closer with Clyde's family. Mother witnessed that closeness and it was even more difficult for her to accept my marriage. I also grew to love Clyde's sisters Marilyn and Mae and their husbands Jack and John. These new siblings comforted me in the turmoil of my blood relatives' hurtful reaction.

Despite how much they didn't want me to be married to Clyde, my parents still wanted me to be part of their lives. Since I didn't know how to cook, and I didn't want to know how to cook, my mother would cook for us. Clyde and I ate dinner at my parent's house at least four or five times a week.

Mother had never seen anybody eat as much as Clyde. She was used to two girls' picky appetites. Daddy used to pay me to eat my vegetables! Yet night after night Clyde and I would attend dinner with Mother and Daddy having strained conversations or uncomfortable silence. I recall one night Daddy poured milk in Clyde's water glass. Unlike other family gatherings there was no laughter, joyful bantering, or familiar friendship being offered at these dinners.

Chapter 9

OUR FIRST FIGHT

I VIVIDLY RECALL OUR first fight. And it happened in public, to Clyde's horror. Clyde had grown up in a quiet, proper English family where if you had a disagreement with someone, you did it privately. I, on the other hand, grew up letting my opinions be known right then and there and at any volume necessary.

The fight happened when Clyde and I went to the main grocery store in Kalamazoo, where we were buying a few items for me to cook. This meant easy to prepare items like cold cereal or cold cuts, for example.

Just as we were checking out, Clyde picked up a ten-cent apple pie and put it on the checkout counter.

"We don't need that!" I told him with authority, a bit of sarcasm in my voice.

"What do you mean we don't need that?" Clyde asked.

"It's too expensive," I retorted, trying to bully my way. "Put it back."

"That's what I want. I love apple pie." Clyde glared at me, biting the words with venom.

"Why don't you put it back?" I told him, rabidly.

By this time the checkout girl was aware of the disagreement and stood there with the pie in her hand waiting to ring it up. She was trying to decide who she should listen to.

Clyde wasn't about to have his new wife tell him what to do. Disgustedly he looked at me, then turned to the checker and said, "I'll be right back."

A whole line of other shoppers had gathered waiting to check out behind me, as I stood there aggravated that Clyde would spend so much money on something so frivolous. Clyde loped to the back of the store where to my horror he picked up eleven more of the same pies and brought them all to the check out counter.

"Ring them all," he told the clerk. She nodded and began ringing each pie.

Clyde paid for our groceries and we headed toward the car, yelling at each other and making a scene. By the time we got home with all those pies, I was beginning to see the humor in the whole thing. We eventually kissed and made up. To this day, Clyde still likes apple pie and I bake them all the time for him.

~

Things remained strained between my parents and me. Gradually they got used to Clyde and saw that he wasn't the evil villain they had imagined. When our parents finally met each other, my parents were impressed with Clyde's mother and father. Mother and Daddy could see that Clyde came from a good and decent home.

Clyde's parents were a very striking couple that met my parents' economic standards. Even though Clyde and I were from totally different religious backgrounds, we had similar lifestyles, morals, and solid family values. My parents were impressed that Clyde's brother, Wes, was the vice president of Spiegel's department store. Clyde's father had retired from being a furnace engineer. Slowly, Mother and Daddy became aware that Clyde wasn't from the wrong side of the tracks. They had pre-judged him for all the wrong reasons.

When Mike, our first child, was born, it was the beginning of a whole new adventure for my parents. The first time my mother saw Mike, she said he was the most beautiful baby ever born. She furnished the nursery with everything. Mother loved for me to meet her in downtown Kalamazoo with the stroller so she could show off her new grandson. Everyone she bragged to agreed with her. Mother knew everybody, and they all had to agree that Mike was an unusually beautiful child, who looked just like his grandfather (Daddy).

When I was pregnant with our second son, Andy, just nineteen months later, Mother and I were walking in downtown Kalamazoo. I saw the most beautiful little boy next to Mike, with dark hair and dark eyes. I wished at that moment that if I were to have a little boy again that he would look just like that.

"What's the little boy's name?" I asked his mother.

"Andy," she replied.

"If I have a little boy, I hope he looks just like your Andy," I told her. "And I'll even name him Andy."

Just a few weeks later, Clyde had gone to his brother-in-law's funeral and I wasn't feeling well enough to accompany him. I had a backache and a toddler to look after. So I stayed home trying to take care of Mike. Our neighbor from upstairs dropped in and asked, "Gerrie, why are things so quiet here today?"

I explained how I was feeling, and she said, "You need

to get to the hospital now!" It's a good thing she insisted, because our second son was born in the hospital elevator! With pitch-black hair, big brown eyes, and a smile to capture all our hearts, we named him Andy.

Mother and Daddy enjoyed the two boys every time they could see them. I became busier and busier as a young mother. By this time, Mother had made it her mission for me to be the perfect wife and mother. As the family grew, it became harder and harder to keep up with what my mother expected of me as a housewife, cooking, cleaning, and mothering.

Clyde, however, was completely satisfied with how I took care of the house and the children. This was a time when Clyde and I had stopped going to church. It was easier not to go than to pack up the kids. Slowly, as we moved away from our church life, we also began quarreling, even about silly things like corn flakes or Rice Krispies.

The disagreements went from minor to major and arguing escalated to where we screamed and yelled at each other every day. I often wondered how we could love each other and hate each other at the same time, but we managed it.

No matter how much we fought, both Clyde and I were good parents. I read countless stories to the boys and Clyde played with them every spare moment he had. Clyde provided well for the family, and we had all the material things we needed. There was no Christian environment, however we were a typical home like millions of other good homes, just trying to make it from one day to the next.

Clyde sold meat for Armor Company and we were transferred to Battle Creek, Michigan, and then to Buffalo, New York. Going from Battle Creek to Buffalo was like falling off the face of the earth. It was bitter, bitter cold. And it seemed even worse because this was the first time in my life that I didn't have a built in babysitter with my mother. I was on my own with two little children and a marriage that was in crisis.

Clyde was at his peak of partying. I didn't think that his parents knew the extent of what was going on in our lives, but out of the blue his mother wrote a letter asking us to watch this new man on TV called Billy Graham.

"He'll be on Saturday night at 8 p.m. on channel 10," she wrote.

Out of respect for Clyde's mother, we both agreed that we would watch the TV show. Church was about the last thing Clyde and I were interested in at that time. We weren't going to church at all and our life was constant conflict.

So on Saturday night at 8 p.m. Clyde turned on channel ten and we watched Billy Graham. I didn't expect much, but I was shocked. He was electrifying, and Clyde and I listened and were drawn to Dr. Graham's message like a magnet.

I perked up especially when I heard Dr. Graham mention that the following week's broadcast would be about men and the kind of husbands they should be. I thought, "Good! That's just what he needs," thinking of all the changes I'd like to see in Clyde and how Dr. Graham might help inspire them. What I didn't know was that he was also going to talk to the wives as well as the husbands the following week.

Clyde and I watched the Billy Graham series that season in Buffalo. I watched for two reasons: one for his mom's benefit, and two because I wanted Clyde to know what a jerk I thought he had been to me.

I recall Dr. Graham signing off by describing that tonight was the hour of decision. I remember going outside afterward and sitting on the front steps. I had an eight-ounce bottle of Coca-Cola in my hand, just sitting on the step, drinking the Coke, and taking in the night air. Clyde joined me on the front porch and we talked about Dr. Graham's message and then we made a decision. We agreed that when we were between forty and forty-six years of age, we would make a decision about God. But at this point our expense account was padded, and we were striving to be on top of the world materialistically. That was far more important than our thoughts about God. We watched Billy Graham several times that month, always promising ourselves that we'd get to the God stuff later when it fit our lifestyle.

But God began dealing with our hearts and a nagging restlessness began. Clyde left Armor Meats to go with another company back in Michigan. We both felt this was a good career move, and it would also take us back near family.

Chapter 10

A New
Turning Point

T HE FIGHTING BETWEEN Clyde and me continued.
Clyde had begun drinking heavily. This caused
even more discord between us. I would resent him
spending money on drinking, so I spent money on myself. I
bought clothes, clothes, and more clothes; things for the children, furnishings for the house, whatever I wanted. Debts
mounted up, which made for even more fighting since there
wasn't enough money to pay for everything and keep up the
lifestyle we had come to expect. Soon Clyde would stop at
the bar after work every night before coming home.

Mother always had gifts waiting. I never had to buy an
article of clothing for any of the children. We had a close
relative who owned a clothing factory and Mother always
came laden with presents of top quality clothing for the children. By this time Mother and Daddy had come to realize
that Clyde was not so bad. But they didn't like his new habit
of heavy drinking.

Our love affair was turning into a nightmare. It was pride
that kept me with Clyde, because my whole family had
predicted that our marriage would fail. I just couldn't walk
out, because it would mean admitting they were right and I

had been wrong. I walked around in circles, ill, as I looked at what was happening in our lives. Clyde was drinking so much his job was even threatened.

Fortunately, God was working on Clyde while he was working on me as well. I didn't know it then, but Clyde had begun evaluating his life.

Clyde was a salesman for a meat company. One day he was driving down an unfamiliar road and was thinking about his life. He was stunned at how his lifestyle didn't measure up to being a Christian at all. Clyde had been contemplating this for several weeks, but that day it was pressing on his heart.

Clyde felt so overwhelmed that he pulled off the road at a small park area and sat down at an empty picnic table. All alone, he tried to sing a song to himself that he had learned as a child, "Oh, How I love Jesus." But the words stuck in Clyde's throat as he realized that he didn't love Jesus and that he hadn't taught our boys the first thing about Jesus. And there, on July 25, 1958, at a roadside table on a rural country road, as reserved as Clyde was, my strong, tall, John Wayne look-alike husband sat down and began to talk to God.

Clyde told me later that he had prayed, "Lord, I don't think I can live the Christian life. My life, my marriage, and my family are broken. But I'm asking You to make me the kind of a man You want me to be."

There at that roadside, Clyde first asked Jesus to come into his life, and forgive him for the lifestyle he'd been living. Clyde prayed, "I don't know if I can be man enough to do all this. So I'm asking You to help me." Clyde had always been a professing Christian, but this time it wasn't just words. He meant it. At that moment, Clyde went from just a *professing* Christian to becoming a true Christian.

The change in him was so drastic so that when he drove into the driveway, I knew something was different before he got out of the car. I remember the scene vividly. I was at the screen door watching the boys play in the front yard. Clyde pulled into the driveway, stopped the car, and walked toward the house. When Clyde put his car keys in his pocket he looked at me, and I knew something was different.

"What happened to you today?" I asked curiously, as he leaned to kiss me hello.

"Can you tell?" Clyde asked surprised.

I said, "Yes, I don't know what, but I can tell something happened." I waved my hands in the air. "It's obvious that something is different."

Clyde sat down on the front porch steps. He looked at his hands, and then up at me. "I gave my heart to the Lord today," he said softly.

"What does that mean?" I demanded.

Clyde thought carefully before he responded, and in a much kinder tone than I was using. "Well, Gerrie, from now on He's number One in my life."

I was offended. "I'm supposed to be number one in your life." I folded my arms, waiting for a response. I was hurt that this was yet another battle to fight. Now it would be over spiritual issues.

Calmly, Clyde looked up and took my hand. "You are number one, Gerrie. But in a different way."

I didn't like the sound of this. It was hard enough to stay with Clyde with all the fighting, but I knew how to do that. I had enjoyed my initial Christian experience, but when we stopped going to church we had drifted away from God. I never doubted that I was a Christian, but there just wasn't time for that with all the other things I had to do. I felt very far away from the Lord. Just because Clyde had a new experience with God didn't mean anything in my life had changed.

Clyde and I were both heavy partiers, and there were not many nights we weren't partying. We were also both heavy smokers. Clyde was a heavy drinker; I was a moderate drinker. My favorite drink was a Slow Gin Fizz, because it tasted like a Cherry Coke. Our marriage was taking a toll from that lifestyle. The people we were running with were not a good influence on either of us.

In shock, I watched Clyde change before my eyes. He picked up a Bible that we had packed away, dusted it off, and began to read it in earnest every night.

On his own, Clyde started helping me with the children. Back in those days it was very uncommon for husbands to help with children's baths or feedings; that was the mother's job. Clyde jumped in to help without even being asked. More amazingly, he quit drinking entirely. The last drink he ever had was that day, July 25, 1958.

We had about thirty-one friends that made up our social circle. They all came over one night expecting a party, when Clyde explained that there would be no drinking in our home anymore after that night. Clyde stood tall in our living room with a bottle of Coke in his hand. The group started to jeer and make smart cracks about Clyde for being "saved."

Clyde looked at them all squarely, "Say all you want, but this is the way it will be in our house. Gerrie and I will not have drinking in our home anymore." Just like that, our friendship abruptly ended with all but two of those friends, Jim and Pat, who accepted our decision and who have remained steadfast friends, even today.

Clyde began going to church without me. It was just fine if he wanted to go, but he wasn't dragging me back with him.

⁓

I'll always be grateful for the love and support of my friend Dorothy Short back then. Dorothy was a strong believer, and our children were the same ages. I loved her personality, and enjoyed her friendship. She was a good ally whenever I'd needed one in the past, so when Clyde became this new fanatic, I went to Dorothy.

Dorothy had been influential as the one Christian example that I knew of outside of Clyde's family. She listened, and encouraged me to go to church with him. That wasn't what I wanted to hear.

I said, "I don't think so." But we started talking on the phone every day, and Dorothy was always so patient and kind. She just kept encouraging me to keep an open mind about going to church with Clyde.

Clyde started taking the boys to Sunday school and left me home. I didn't mind if he wanted to take them, but he got them dressed by himself. I was so unhappy with our life then, that looking back at it, you would think that I would have appreciated this new decision Clyde had made. But I didn't appreciate it one bit. I felt threatened and isolated.

Finally, with the encouragement from Dorothy, I decided to go with him to church. But truthfully, the only reason I agreed to go was to keep up appearances.

"At least this way my children will look presentable," I told Dorothy over the phone. "I'm tired of seeing them leave for church with their Healthtex t-shirts on inside out. This Sunday they'll get there with the snaps on the right side."

That first Sunday back to church was amazing. It was my first time at this church and an evangelist was speaking. Clyde took me up to the balcony and every time the pastor spoke, he put his hand up toward the balcony.

A couple of times, I was just sure he was talking to me personally, "Mothers, where have your children heard the name of Jesus? Profanity or Bible story?" he asked. I swallowed a big lump in my throat. It hadn't been either from me.

I was just sure Dorothy had tipped him off that I was coming. And I was hurt and angry that she had set me up this way. When at the end of the sermon the pastor asked people to come forward, I got up and walked out the door, and it slammed behind me. I didn't intend for it to slam, but it did just the same.

Clyde was angry. He ran out after me and grabbed me by the arm. "What are you doing?" Clyde asked me in a hushed whisper. I was mad at him. I jerked my hand away and stomped toward the car. Clyde came after me and we drove away consumed by the anger of the moment—in our rage we forgot the children in Sunday school! When I realized what we'd done, that made me even madder. Now, we had to go back there.

That day, God began working in my heart. I was angry, but Dorothy assured me that she had nothing to do with the pastor's message that morning. Despite my hurt and anger, I couldn't stop thinking about all the things the evangelist said.

A couple weeks later, the boys were napping and I was doing the dishes. I was up to my elbows in Ivory Liquid soapsuds when I asked myself, "Gerrie, why are you being so stubborn?"

I thought about that for a minute, then I said to myself,

"What Clyde is now, is exactly what you both need. Now you're the one holding out."

I got on my knees in the kitchen with soapsuds all over my hands and I told the Lord I was so sorry for the way I had been. With tears in my eyes I said, "Lord, I want to make things right. Please help me. I don't know how."

I didn't tell Clyde about my prayer, but I did tell Dorothy.

After about a week, Clyde noticed that I was different. We began going to church together and our love sparked anew. It was like falling in love all over again.

What Clyde and I didn't know was that the pastor of our church had called all the deacons together. He told them that there was a nice young couple with two small children who were really involved in the party scene. He explained that this young couple would require a lot of fellowship to make a real lifestyle change that would please God. He challenged the group to make sure that Clyde and I were invited to one of their homes every night after Sunday night church.

Clyde and I began accepting these invitations. And remarkably, God replaced those thirty-one friends who left us with many more beautiful lives. Our new friends were strong believers with good moral values, seeking to please God. Pretty soon Sunday nights started also becoming Friday nights, and then Friday, Saturday, and Sunday nights were booked with this group. It seemed as if all of us—Clyde and I, and our new friends—were all having so much fun in our fellowship.

Then I became sick. When I realized I was pregnant for the third time Clyde and I worried about how we would explain to our new friends that loved to get together so often that we would have to curtail our gatherings because I was too ill from the pregnancy. We were so concerned that they would be disappointed, but I just couldn't keep up the pace.

So Clyde announced at one of our parties that we were going to have to eliminate some of our get-togethers. First the group grew silent and Clyde and I exchanged a worried frown. But then, in unison they all went "Whew!"

That was when we found out how the pastor had told them to look after us. I wouldn't be writing this book without the support and time they invested in our lives. Clyde and I have used that same principle of investing time in other people during all our years of ministry.

We cut back on the social gathering, but I still made time for my new friends. I couldn't get enough of the support from my new church family. I was now surrounded by people who did everything they could to help one another. I learned how to serve by watching them. And by watching them, I learned to care for someone else other than myself.

I was expecting this third baby when Mike was five Andy was three-and-a-half, and this time surrounded by a loving, supportive church family. By now Mother and Daddy had come to accept Clyde as the good man that he was. Because my father had two girls he made it known that this time he wanted a granddaughter.

When our daughter Lori was born after a lengthy labor, Clyde went over to the house at 4:30 a.m. to wake Mother and Daddy with the news. Daddy was so excited he could barely bring himself to believe he had a granddaughter. "It's a girl?" he asked Clyde repeatedly. After assuring Daddy that baby number three was indeed a girl, Daddy continued to ask. Finally Clyde teased him, "No, it's a boy." Daddy sighed in exasperation and Clyde couldn't tease him again. He convinced Daddy that we really did have a baby girl. Daddy ran around the neighborhood at five in the morning, waking the neighbors in celebration.

As the family expanded, Clyde and I wanted to own our own home. We'd been renting a small house, but we decided to try to buy a house. Clyde landed a second a job at a brand new restaurant called McDonald's. When he would get through working at one job he would go right in there to work. We saved every cent from the McDonald's job to put toward buying our own home.

One day my folks came and offered to help us financially to buy a home. But as usual with Mother, there were conditions on the loan. They wanted to help us, if we would "drop some of this religious stuff."

"Religious stuff?" I asked. "Like what are you referring to?"

Mother explained, "Well, you don't need to go to your church every Sunday morning, and every Sunday night, and every Wednesday night, too."

While this seemed like a reasonable request to them, they didn't understand that Clyde and I could hardly wait to get to church. We were attending for practical reasons, as well as spiritual ones. We eagerly attended church services to learn how to be better parents, better marriage partners, better neighbors, and better believers. Our hearts were open to be taught and we eagerly anticipated every service.

Their offer just made us stronger in our faith. As graciously as we could, we turned them down. Clyde and I were determined to practice what we believed to be right for our family, even if it meant waiting longer to buy our home.

Our fourth child, Tim, was a very sick child from birth. At about two-months-old he didn't respond with normal reflexes, like grabbing a finger. He was lethargic and not thriving the way a normal baby should. Tim suffered one fever after another, and nothing worked to get him well.

Tim was in and out of the hospital many times when doctors came to the conclusion that he had Cystic Fibrosis, and put him on food for Cystic Fibrosis patients. They cautioned Clyde and me that he might be mildly retarded. It was our darkest day.

With four children, ages six, four, two, and an infant, and a house to care for, I tried to keep the house nice, but it didn't meet my mother's standards. Everything always had to be ready just in case one of my aunts happened to "stop by." Mother was obsessed with my housekeeping and made me feel guilty if everything didn't meet her specifications. She wanted my home to be picture perfect so that if one of the relatives walked in they would exclaim to the neighbors, "Oh, isn't she amazing, being able to keep a house like this with four small children?"

Even as adults, Bedonna and I never met Mother's expectations regarding our weight. Each time Mother would see us, she would pinch Bedonna's midriff or my backside and sniff in disgust. After we had been properly admonished for being too heavy, Mother would bring out warm chocolate chip cookies or fresh brownies to tempt us.

One Thanksgiving I remember having climbed to 128 pounds, and Mother noted how "fat" I was, scolding me for not being thin. "Look at the size of your tukus!" she exclaimed. Then she put a large dollop of turkey stuffing on my plate and said, "Eat! Eat! Eat!"

When Mother walked into my house it was white glove inspection time. She inspected the moldings, the toilets, and the top of the refrigerator. She noticed if the furniture needed polishing, if the front porch needed to be swept, and if there were any clothes needing to be hung up. Despite the fact that I had four small children, she honestly believed that all toys should be picked up and put in the toy box whenever the children weren't playing with them. And she wanted me to tend to all these details, even when I was too exhausted even to pick up my foot.

To "help" me, Mother would make lists of tasks I needed to accomplish. It was pride for her. She wanted me to look like I had a housekeeper when I was just trying to keep sane. Mother would make lists that included things like defrosting the refrigerator, cleaning the oven, polishing the silver, vacuuming, dusting, window washing...the lists would go on and on.

"Just do what you can on the list," Mother would tell me. "You never know when one of your aunts might drop by."

This went on repeatedly. Because I had embarrassed her so much by marrying Clyde, I wanted to please her and have her approval. And even though I'd get mad at her, I'd still work on her lists and try to make her happy. I was so exhausted from caring for the children that it was easier to just agree to do the list than to argue with her that I didn't have time or energy.

One day, Clyde came home and found a long list on the dining room table. He asked, "What is this list? Who is this for?"

I told him, with tears filling my eyes, "Mother came over and left this list for me to do, so the house would look nice. Just in case somebody stopped in. She told me, 'Gerrie, this is what your house needs to look like.'"

Clyde grabbed the list and stormed out. He went directly to my mother's house, demanding to know why she had done something so outrageous. He told her in no uncertain terms not to ever do anything like this again. That was the end of my mother's lists.

Our son Tim's condition continued to deteriorate. We took him from doctor to doctor, trying to find someone who could help us. Finally, another doctor examined him and sent us to a specialist. The specialist felt that Tim's condition was from allergies and not Cystic Fibrosis. Sure enough, it proved to be true. Another doctor suggested that because of Tim's serious skin conditions, perhaps a cooler, more humid climate in the East would be better for him. Clyde and I sighed. We couldn't just pack up and go. But God had a plan.

Clyde's brother Wes, the vice president of Spiegel's department store, called Clyde one day with a proposition, not knowing anything about Tim's new diagnosis.

"Clyde," Wes said, "we're looking for an executive at one of the companies that manufacture Spiegel shoes. It's called Songo Shoe Manufacturing Corporation."

A close friend of Wes, a man named Abe Berkowitz, owned the company. Abe was a Jew and an empire builder. Wes's son, Wes Jr. who was Clyde's age, was working there and he needed trustworthy additional help.

Imagine this coming to us just two days after the doctor recommended a move to the East for Tim! Here Clyde and I thought moving east was an impossibility. And now we were handed an opportunity to do just that. So we sold the house, packed everything up, and went off to Portland, Maine.

Chapter 11

WELCOME TO PORTLAND, MAINE

E LOVED PORTLAND! It took awhile, but we loved it. The people there were so nice to us. Most of them were trying to figure out my outgoing personality, fashion style, and how I would fit into their conservative New England culture. But after a few months they all seemed to decide that I was OK, and many became loyal friends.

Tim improved remarkably, and at nine months he sat up for the first time. This was a miracle, from how he had been and as we continued our life in Portland, Tim continued to improve. We found out later that Tim was allergic to the water in Michigan. His motor skills were a bit behind, but he began walking at eighteen months. He grew to be a perfectly normal little boy.

We bought an old Victorian house on Pitt Street in Portland. It was a three-story, rambling Victorian, and it was historically beautiful. There was a big barn in the backyard and as we became more and more involved with the young people in our church it was clear to me that they needed a place to hang out on weekends.

I kept thinking about how we had this big beautiful hip roof barn that would work perfectly. It was a city barn with two stories, painted to match the house with a big window on the second floor that originally was used for hay loading and unloading. So one day we had all the young people come over, and they helped us clean out the barn by tossing debris out that very window.

Then I went to work and converted the barn over to a youth center. I called the Pepsi Company and asked them to donate the sodas on the weekends, which they did. I contacted the potato chip company to do the same. A restaurant going out of business donated all their booths, which made a great lounging area. Somebody else built a snack bar. The candy distributor and potato chip company brought us candy and chips to sell every week. The horse stalls were made into a bowling alley. Each week we would have a different speaker for the young people to challenge them in their faith. We saw amazing growth in the teens of the church and many of them went on to study for the ministry.

The church young people loved The Barn, as we called it, and enjoyed many great times interacting with the group. As Tim began to develop a personality, he became exceedingly stubborn. So much so that one of our missionaries prayed that Tim would come to know the Lord at a very young age. With a ministry in our backyard, and a wide variety of support people to run it, our children had many opportunities to see God at work. By having The Barn, it helped to establish our children in understanding the importance of serving the Lord. There was the excitement of young people developing their faith. Back then, you didn't boldly witness to others, you simply shared the importance of living the life of a Christian.

I watched my brother-in-law Wes, a prominent Chicago businessman, take advantage of every opportunity to share his faith. While others had a bar in their offices, Wes had a gold-plated water cooler. He felt that God had put him in his position of business because God had a plan for him. Wes would tell me that God put Clyde and I where we were to do the same.

Wes called every week and had something to share about how God was working in his life and in the lives of those he worked with. As a high-ranking executive, Wes had an opportunity to meet many others in power. When Billy Graham held a crusade in Chicago, Wes was asked to be chairman of that event. He was a very sophisticated, distinguished man, with a passion for life and a magnetic personality.

Each week when Wes called he would encourage me to share Jesus and what He had done for us with my neighbors. I loved to share everything with them. One by one, two by two, they came to know the same Lord and Savior I knew.

One of the things the neighbors could see was how God protected our children. Our home sat across the street from a house that belonged to the church. One day, our daughter Lori was playing out by the driveway. Tim was playing at the bottom of the driveway with a little girl from our neighborhood. It was a long, sloped drive and at the bottom was a rock on one side and a tree on the other. Lori got into the car and in child's play somehow released the brake. When she got out of the car it began to roll and ran right over her foot! Then it continued rolling down the hill toward Tim and the neighbor girl who didn't see it coming, and were too young to know what to do if they had. Just as the car got to them, the neighbor girl pulled Tim out of the way. The car rolled past the children and right between the tree and the rock. It stopped at the front porch of the house across the street, which belonged to the church. The porch was a bit battered, but the children were unharmed.

Since it was our church property that was damaged, no one was a bit concerned about the damage to the porch. But what everyone was aware of was that miracles happened that day. Lori had her foot examined and the physician found no damage. Tim's life and the life of the young girl he was playing with were both spared. Our neighbor was outside and saw the incident unfold before her eyes and fainted. Clyde and I were glancing out the window when it happened, helplessly watching, knowing there was nothing we could do. Yet Clyde and I knew that the entire incident was evidence of God's protection.

~

Late one autumn while living in Portland, I woke up violently ill. I was rushed to the doctor to learn that I had contracted mumps meningitis, a complicated virus. I was able to recover, but not without mounting doctor bills and expensive medication. As Christmas neared, and I recovered, my biggest concern wasn't my health, but how I could get presents for the children. Christmas was so important to me. I'd missed so many celebrations of our Lord's birth when I grew up, I wanted every Christmas to be memorable for my children.

I knew the children would receive gifts from their grandparents and our friends, but I wanted the children to have toys for Christmas from Clyde and me. I asked God to provide some way for our children to have a memorable Christmas despite having no money.

Clyde and I had been renovating rooms in our house, and he decided to remove the linoleum in a back bedroom. It was old, cracked, and yellow, with an ugly flowered pattern. When he pulled the corner of the old linoleum back toward the center of the room, Clyde was astounded to find six five-dollar bills. It was enough money to buy each of the children something fun to open on Christmas morning from Mommy and Daddy.

My Jewish cousins, Goldie and Barney, came from Michigan to visit us in Portland. This was the couple that I had stayed with in Detroit right after graduation. One night after everyone went to sleep, my cousin Goldie and I started talking about spiritual matters.

We tiptoed into the bathroom where we could talk and not wake anyone. I told Goldie, "I'll show you in the Bible the questions you're asking me." She had been asking me questions about why my faith was so strong. Goldie sat on the edge of the tub and I sat on the toilet seat. We were both dressed in our pajamas, with our bathrobes and slippers.

With my Bible in my lap, Goldie challenged me, "You show me those verses where they were told about Jesus in the Old Testament and I'll believe it."

I looked at Goldie in wonder. "You'll believe it if I show you?" I whispered to her, as I pulled my Bible up to my chest.

"I can't imagine it being in the Old Testament, but you show me and I'll believe it," Goldie confirmed, folding one leg over the other and crossing her arms.

So I showed her the verse in Micah 5:2 which tells that Jesus would be born in Bethlehem. I read out loud to her, "But you, O Bethlehem Ephrathah, are only a small village among all the people of Judah. Yet a ruler of Israel will come from you, one whose origins are from the distant past."

Goldie looked at me with her eyes so wide in silence and disbelief. "I don't believe it," she said, "What else is there? You show me and I'll believe it."

"Okay," I told her, "It says He'll be born of a virgin." I turned to Isaiah 7:14 and read, "All right then, the Lord himself will give you the sign. Look! The virgin will conceive a child! She will give birth to a son and will call him Immanuel (which means 'God is with us')."

Goldie's mouth dropped open. "I don't believe it!" she exclaimed. "What else have you got?" Goldie wanted to know, squirming on the edge of the tub. So I showed her Psalm 22:1, another passage from the Old Testament, "My God, my God, why have you abandoned me? Why are you so far away when I groan for help?" These same verses are also found in Matthew 46 and Mark 15. It is the same verse that Jesus quoted while hanging on the cross.

Goldie's eyes widened and she threw her hands in the air. "I don't believe it!" she cried. And she didn't.

As kindly as I could, I told Goldie, "It's not that you don't believe it; it's that you won't believe it. You tell me you wish you had a faith like mine. Goldie, you can. It's a choice you have to make. I can't make it for you."

Goldie was astounded and knew what I had told her was true. She looked at me and she was speechless. I picked up my Bible and we left the bathroom, tiptoeing back to our bedrooms. I knew Goldie had a lot to think about.

Chapter 12

Called of the Lord—
On the Same Day

IN Portland, Clyde worked long, long hours. He would get up at 5:30 a.m. and read his Bible before he went to work. He began each day asking God to bless his day, and to be used by God. After I had the children off to school, I would settle in my favorite spot on the sofa and read my devotion book and Bible each day.

One morning Clyde picked up his Bible and opened to Matthew 4:19, "And he saith unto them, Follow me, and I will make you fishers of men." Clyde told me it felt as if it said to him, "Drop those nets, follow Me" (kjv).

"Gerrie," he explained later, "it said, 'Clyde, drop those shoes you love so much, and follow Me. I will make you to become a fisher of men.' I don't know how to explain it, except that the Scripture was speaking to me," he told me.

While this message came to Clyde, and unbeknown to me that this took place in his life, I was having my daily devotions. I opened to page sixty-four in a book titled *My Utmost for His Highest*. It's an old devotional book by Oswald Chambers. Today, as I read my copy, I am struck by the pull of the words. They came as if they were from God's heart to my heart.

The lesson was on Acts 20:24, "But my life is worth nothing to me unless I use it for finishing the work assigned me by the Lord Jesus." The devotion commentary read, "It is easier to serve God without a vision, easier to work for God without a call, because then you are not bothered by what God requires."[1] In this lesson the apostle Paul says he counted his life dear only in order that he might fulfill the ministry that he had received. He refused to use his energy for any other thing than giving out the Gospel that he had received.

The words jumped off the page and wrapped around my heart. This time the meaning of the passage was different than ever before. My heart was racing. I remember it vividly; I was sitting on my brown sofa, sipping my coffee. And it was as if the words were spoken by God, "Gerrie, I want you to serve Me with your entire life, all your energy, and your entire heart. Just as Paul served Me with all the energy he had, I want you to serve Me as well."

I felt God continuing, "The apostle Paul refused to use his energy for anything other than giving out the Gospel."

Oops! People always complimented me on my energy, and I liked using it for God. I was using my energy for Christian service, but I couldn't imagine leaving everything behind to do it. This verse was speaking to me that I wasn't as willing to leave all as I thought, if that was what God required. I liked serving God right where I was, doing everything I could right there. I thought I was very useful to God right there in Portland. But that wasn't putting Jesus as my Guide as to where I should go. I felt like God was speaking to me in a new, different way. But why would He do that, when I was already doing everything I could to serve Him?

It was my own judgment as to where I would be of most use to God. What bothered me most were questions that God might be telling me that all the energy I was using was good, but that He might have other ways for me to use it in full-time Christian service. This meant abandoning everything we had worked for. How could I do that with four small children?

"Could this be true of me?" I gasped.

God spoke to me in a very unique way, different than I had ever experienced before that. I was stunned and puzzled over what this meant. How did this apply to me? I knew I had never felt this way before. And I did not dream that Clyde had had a similar experience that same morning.

We took turns going to the midweek service. Clyde would go one week, and I would stay home with the children. Then the next week, I would go to the service and Clyde would look after the children. That night, Clyde stayed home to keep working on the sample tags for the new shoes to be made. He kept thinking of how God had spoken to him that morning and instead of fishing for fish, God wanted him to fish for men. Clyde wondered if instead of working with shoe soles, perhaps God wanted him to fish for men's souls.

I rode home with my pastor, talking about a couple who had gone into the mission field.

"Don't you think she just did that for him?" I asked. Pastor quietly turned his head just a little bit. He spoke over his shoulder to me in the backseat, "Gerrie, God doesn't call one without the other. He needs a team."

That was music to my ears. If God was calling me, that relieved me of that responsibility. But I had my doubts. Why would God want a mother with four children, and a husband like Clyde who didn't like to study?

When I came home that evening, Clyde was waiting at our big Victorian glass door. When he opened the door he had that concerned look, like maybe I was spending too much money.

Clyde said, "Sit down Gerrie, I need to talk to you."

I took off my coat, tossed it over the back of a chair, and sat down on the sofa. I didn't know what was coming, but from the frown on Clyde's face I didn't think it was going to be good.

"Gerrie, I don't understand this myself," Clyde began, "but I believe God is speaking to me differently than He ever has before."

With my heart in my throat, I was gasping inside, "Oh my, what's happening?" I said to myself. I shared what happened to me that same day during my devotions. Together we began to feel the call of God in our hearts and in our minds.

Both of us recalled a few months prior when two missionaries were at our house. These two women both had been missionaries in China in World War II and were captured. They had the most amazing and inspiring stories how God had sustained them in a Nazi concentration camp.

Miss Brownsburg, who spoke in a whisper from having her vocal chords damaged, said God gave her a song to sing. Katarina was a nurse in the same concentration camp and took care of Miss Brownsburg. They were still serving the Lord and had moved to Portland, Maine. Friends of our pastor had helped them get reestablished. As I got to know them I wanted others that we knew to hear some of their miraculous stories.

So I invited everybody, business colleagues, neighbors, and other friends to our home to hear their incredible story. We moved a lot of the antiques around, pushed the furniture back, and brought in chairs. The house was lined up wall-to-wall with people all the way around. They had to listen ever so attentively due to Miss Brownsburg's quiet voice. After she finished her stories, she looked at Clyde and me and said, "Clyde and Gerrie, we've never heard your testimonies. Why don't you share them with us now?"

I didn't hesitate to share one-on-one with somebody, but not to everyone we knew at the same time. Clyde looked at me with the most fearful look I'd ever seen, and said, "Go ahead, Gerrie."

When I get nervous, the volume of my voice goes up. So in a loud, strangled voice, I said the first thing that came into my head, and somehow I got through how I came to know the Lord.

Then I looked at Clyde with a mischievous twinkle in my eye and said, "Go ahead, Clyde." While coughing continuously and with his nose running, Clyde somehow managed to express his testimony.

In her very quiet voice Miss Brownsburg said, "Thank you. Perhaps God will see fit to use you in His ministry some day."

Before I could stop myself I said in a voice much too loud, especially compared to her soft, barely audible voice, "God needs Christian businessmen as much as he needs ministers." There was dead silence in the room.

I began serving refreshments and Miss Brownsburg and Katarina asked to be taken home. The wonderful evening had turned uncomfortable and awkward. Everyone was listening as they said good-bye. Clyde helped them both on with their coats, escorted them to our car, and drove them home. I kept serving refreshments wondering, "What happened?"

When Clyde came back I was looking for him. "Did they say anything?" I asked him.

Clyde replied grinning, "They didn't need to, Gerrie, you said it all."

By the time Clyde and I realized that we had received the call from God, it was late at night. But even though it was so late, we called our pastor and his wife. They came right over. They told us they had been praying for this very thing to occur. In fact, they had been praying with Miss Brownsburg and Katarina.

My first reaction was, "Why us? Why Clyde and Gerrie, with four small children and a thriving business?" We loved and enjoyed every day of our lives in Portland. We loved the relationship we had with Wes and Carolyn and their children. We loved our house, our neighbors, and our church. We loved Portland, our lifestyle, the smell of the pine, the snowy winters, the brilliant fall colors, all four of our children's thriving health. There was nothing in Portland that we wanted to leave. Clyde loved the business of making shoes, and enjoyed a large office overlooking the Back Bay.

Clyde and I both knew the call from God was real, but there were so many things we didn't understand. We talked with Pastor and his wife until late into the night. I felt encouraged, but not convinced. Still doubtful, they prayed for God to make it ever so clear to both Clyde and me that this call was truly from Him. They prayed that we would not have any doubts.

In order for Clyde to enter the ministry, he would need to attend Bible college. This would be a financial burden for two reasons: Bible colleges cost money to attend, and Clyde would have to work at a much lower paying job to support us.

To raise the funds, we knew we would have to say good-bye to our beautiful Victorian house. We could sell our large collection of antiques, which would allow us to pay off our debts including enormous doctor bills.

And then two things happened.

Twenty-four hours after we had prayed for God to show us a sign that we were really to go to Bible college, we received a fifty cent rebate from when I paid to renew my driver's license. I recognized this as the first money God provided to support our call and I knew God would provide the rest we needed as well.

I called my parents to tell them what we were planning to do and that was almost as bad as when they found out I was a believer. Clyde wanted to attend Bible college in Grand Rapids, Michigan, about seventy miles from Kalamazoo where they still lived. But Mother and Daddy did not want us to come back to Michigan. They were so upset that Clyde would leave a profitable business, a promising career, and a beautiful home, and take four children to study to prepare for the ministry.

A few days later the second thing happened. I received a postcard from my father that was just the encouragement I needed. He said:

> Dear children,
>
> Just a line to say all is OK at home. A bit bewildered about it all, but I can assure you not confused. I'm at a loss to know how you two will be able to accomplish so much in such a little time. Naturally the big obstacle is your debt to the credit union. But you both seem so positive that you can mount it. Time will tell. I'm positive that he will make the grade.
>
> All my love to you dear, the children, and Clyde.

When Daddy sent this card, it was the green light for me to go. I now wanted to go with all my heart.

I loved all my things, and I loved all my friends, but now I could part with them. And God began to supply whatever we needed in the most unusual ways.

Chapter 13

BIBLE COLLEGE, HERE WE COME

OING OFF TO Bible college was a challenge. Clyde was not a "student" of the Bible. He was terrified that he might not measure up as a Bible scholar. What he enjoyed reading most each morning was a few verses out of his Bible, followed by the sports page.

While my parents were not supportive of our call into the ministry, neither were Clyde's. In fact, Clyde's father wrote a scorching letter of four pages, admonishing Clyde for leaving a prominent position. It crushed Clyde, but he had no second thoughts. He knew that God was calling.

Two days later, Clyde's brother Wes wrote a letter to Clyde. Wes was the brother who was responsible for promoting Clyde to his position. Wes had a great deal of money and trust invested in Clyde. I was afraid for Clyde to open the letter. If Clyde's father had been so upset, imagine what Wes's letter would say.

But Wes's letter was the complete opposite of his father's. Wes wrote how proud and thrilled he was that God had called his baby brother into an avenue of ministry. He didn't know what it would be, but he was happy for us. He wrote how much he loved us, and promised to pray for our ministry.

Out of all the people that could possibly support us, for Clyde and me to have Wes's endorsement gave new power to our commitment and desire. Between my father's card and Wes's encouragement, I had a new attitude.

But the big problem for Clyde was how to tell Mr. Berkowitz, the owner of the shoe company. "Mr. B" was not known for an even disposition. His whole life revolved around the business. He was known to go into a rage if he found a rubber band on the floor of the factory. To make sure he got his money's worth on the salaries, he had Wes check the factory on one Sunday and Clyde the other; and Sunday was their only day off.

Mr. B. and Wes were friends, and Spiegel's was one of their large accounts. But friendship wouldn't stop him from going into a rage when he found out that Clyde was going to leave the firm.

Mr. Berkowitz had challenged Clyde's ethics more than once. One of the situations that arose was that he wanted Clyde to lie to an account that shoes had been shipped, when in fact they had just begun the order. He told Clyde to tell them the order was "on the way."

Clyde refused.

"I'm sorry, Mr. Berkowitz, I can't do that." Clyde explained firmly. "I can't lie."

Mr. Berkowitz went crazy. "Either you lie or go into the ministry or something!" he shouted, not having any idea that God had called us.

Clyde just kept waiting for the right timing to tell Mr. Berkowitz that he would be leaving the company.

Now it was almost Christmas bonus time and I wanted Clyde to wait to tell Mr. B. that he would be going to Michigan to Bible college until after our bonus check arrived. It was hard to know what was ahead for us financially, and I knew that bonus check would be important. But Clyde felt it was only right to tell him ahead of time.

Clyde approached Mr. B. in his office and told him he had something important to tell him. Carefully, Clyde proceeded to tell his boss that God had spoken to his heart about leaving the business and going into the ministry.

Clyde waited for the explosion, but instead Mr. Berkowitz just stared at him. Then, in his Yiddish accent, he replied reproachfully, "Clyde, what can I say? If it was anything else, I wouldn't be at a loss for words. But I wish you the best." He extended his hand in friendship. He continued, "And if it doesn't work out, you always have a job waiting here for you."

And yes, Mr. Berkowitz gave us a generous Christmas bonus that final year.

Chapter 14

Saying Good-bye
to Portland

BEFORE WE LEFT Portland, we were asked to speak at our church. I can remember the day well. I was all dressed up and I even wore gloves, trying to look especially nice. As we shared how God had been working in our lives, saying good-bye to everybody, people started pressing money in our hands, and in Clyde's pockets. When we got home, we felt embarrassed that we had so much money. There were people there that we could have been helping.

Money seemed to come in from all over. A couple came by and told us, "We've been saving this money to redecorate our home." They pressed an envelope into Clyde's hand. We emphatically said, "No!" But before we could protest further they insisted. They wanted to be part of our call. Years later they were richly blessed when they inherited a huge sum of money from a relative they didn't know they had in England. A friend of our pastor's wife heard that both Clyde and I were called of the Lord on the same day, and although she had never met us, she wanted to send one hundred dollars for us to use however we needed it.

Our large Victorian home sold in one day. Clyde and I were overwhelmed with the generosity of our community. We felt like we had too much money to leave with. There was cash in our pockets, my purse, and even my gloves.

But God knew it was just the right amount.

As we were loading everything up for the final trip, Wes Jr. and Carolyn came up and handed us a new Phillips translation Bible. Everything had already been packed tight, so we just put the Bible on the dashboard of the car.

That was the first time I cried because I was leaving everything material that I counted dear. I loved our friends, our church, our pastor, and our home. I loved Wes Jr. and Carolyn and our antiques. There was nothing I didn't love in Portland, Maine.

We started out—four little children in the back seat, Clyde and me in the front, and drove about two hundred miles that day to Worcester, Massachusetts, until the car started sputtering, choking, and died. It was December 27, 1962, and the icy winds were whining in the air.

Clyde took the Bible off the dashboard and opened it up to the words of 1 Peter 1:7, "These trials will show that your faith is genuine. It is being tested as fire tests and purifies gold—though your faith is far more precious than mere gold. So when your faith remains strong through many trials, it will bring you much praise and glory and honor on the day when Jesus Christ is revealed to the whole world." I knew it was from God. I can't say I was thankful that the car had broken down, especially with four kids in the back seat, on a cold, winter day, in a strange city, and with limited funds. I knew that God showed us that verse, but truthfully, at that point, silver and gold looked a lot better than trials.

Clyde wasn't sure what to do next. We had to figure out if the car could be salvaged, but to do that it would have to be towed. Fortunately, as the car was breathing its last breath, Clyde was able to pull off the highway near a Howard Johnson Restaurant. He remembered meeting a business colleague's father, a Mr. von Hozzel, two weeks earlier. It was a brief, chance meeting at his office. Clyde remembered that Mr. von Hozzel lived in Worcester, and he asked me to see if I could find Mr. von Hozzel's name in the phone book.

When I went in to look it up, I called our pastor first. I was so scared and I told our pastor that I wanted to come home. "This just isn't for me," I cried.

But to my shock, he crushed me beyond description. In what sounded cold and cruel he said, "Gerrie, you no longer belong to us. You're going to have to see what God has for you in this dire circumstance."

I was shaken. As I hung up the phone, I wiped my eyes and blew my nose into my soggy Kleenex. I couldn't believe that my devoted pastor would feel this way. I didn't understand that God had a solution. This one seemed too big for God.

I looked up Mr. von Hozzel's number for Clyde and Clyde contacted this man. His wife answered, and told Clyde that her husband was out antiquing and that she had no idea where he was.

Things got worse. When Clyde called for a tow truck, the driver informed us that Clyde could ride in the tow truck, but not the children or me. What were we going to do? We had no car, and it was a freezing, blustery cold New England evening.

As Clyde was negotiating with the tow truck driver and trying to figure out what to do, this brand new, big, long, sleek black Cadillac drove into the entrance of the restaurant. He drove right up to Clyde. It was Mr. von Hozzel! His wife had contacted him. He rolled down his window and offered to do whatever he could to help.

Mr. von Hozzel said he'd take the children and me to his house, and told the tow truck driver to drop Clyde off there as well.

"Don't worry," he said to me sympathetically, "we'll figure it out."

Mr. von Hozzel was an influential man in his community and said he'd see about finding a new car. What we thought was too much money, when we left Portland, was exactly the right amount to purchase a thoroughly used Ford sedan. And even though you couldn't purchase cars on a Sunday in those days, Mr. von Hozzel made it possible for us to do so.

I can still remember putting the four children on the countertop in the von Hozzel kitchen. Mrs. von Hozzel gave them all ice cream cones, and then helped me clean them up. She had never even met me before, and she opened her home to our family. We slept at the von Hozzel house that night. And the next morning, when we were ready to get back on the road in our "new" used Ford, she packed a huge lunch for the entire family. She put it in the car as we were leaving with her warm wishes for success as we drove away. To this day, I think of her as my angel on that day.

Clyde and I started out in awe of God taking care of our needs. I could see what the pastor meant when he told me that I didn't belong to him. I had to rely on God. And I was honored that I had been called to see Him work His miracles in our lives.

The kids were settled in the backseat and as we were driving down the road, I noticed there was a long cord hanging from the dashboard.

"I wonder what that fits into," Clyde commented. I should tell you that Clyde is the least mechanically minded man I've ever known. But even so, he kept trying to fit that cord into the dashboard.

"I think it might be the radio," he said enthusiastically. He kept fiddling with it, until at last he pushed the cord into the right socket. On came the radio! And it was George Beverly Shea singing "How Great Thou Art." There were two wet faces and four filled eyes in that front seat as the kids wanted to know why we were crying. Triumphantly, their Daddy explained how God used that old beat up car and a funny cord to provide for us since we couldn't go to church that morning.

"We'll have church in the car!" Mike exclaimed, and the rest of the kids cheered.

The rest of trip to Kalamazoo was uneventful. But when we drove into my parents' driveway, the old car died, never to start again. My father was in the car business and found another old car for us. And from that day through the end of Bible college, one car would die and Daddy would come up with another one.

Mother and Daddy were so disappointed that Clyde was leaving a successful business, and embarrassed that he was going into the ministry to live in poverty. Mother had said, "If you have to go to Bible college, go any place, but don't come back to Michigan!" It was more humiliation for them to endure.

When I told them that God was leading us to a Bible college fewer than one hundred miles from their home, Mother and Daddy had a change of heart. They were so glad to have grandchildren close again. But they did not tell anyone for quite some time why we were really going to Grand Rapids. They just let the family and neighbors think we were working for Hush Puppy shoe manufacturing in Grand Rapids for the first couple of years.

Chapter 15

GETTING STARTED
IN GRAND RAPIDS

WHEN CLYDE WENT to find us a place to live in Grand Rapids what he found was the extreme opposite of what we left in Portland, Maine. All we could afford was a small flat on the second floor of an old, battered apartment building. It had a space heater for combating the cold winters, and a tiny kitchen with a stove that I had to push a chair up against to hold the oven door shut. There were curtains for interior doors, but it was in our price range, and since we didn't know what would happen in the future, I knew it was the best Clyde could find.

Being consigned to the arrangement didn't mean I liked it. In fact, I didn't like it much at all. When mother came up to see where we were going to be living, she was extremely upset. I began showing her all the positive things about the place and before long, I had convinced myself. It was close to shopping, it had three bedrooms, it was very clean, warm, and it was a roof over our heads. It honestly wasn't much more than that, but it was home and we were happy there.

As Clyde began Bible college, so many good things happened I don't even remember the ugliness anymore. I just remember how God worked in our lives back then.

It has never taken me long to make new friends, and Grand Rapids was no exception. Clyde went to school full time and also held a full-time job. The first time he brought the family to our new home, we walked up this long, steep flight of stairs. At the top of the stairs, right at our front door, were all kinds of groceries. Bags of flour and sugar, spices, macaroni, rice, bread, cheese, milk, juice, and even a six-pack of Coke! There were special treats for the children tucked in the bags, too, such as cookies, candy, and popcorn. The note said it was from my cousins, who I called "Aunt Lynn and Uncle Joe." It was the first of many warm greetings and encouragement from them. Uncle Joe, my father's nephew, was the most like my father of any of the relatives. I knew he was looking out for us, because he and Daddy had a close relationship.

I made up my mind that while Clyde was in school, I was not going to complain (even though I'd want to). I knew it wouldn't have taken much for Clyde to be discouraged with the load he carried. I tried to look for the positive and longed for the day when we'd have a home again. Trying to take care of four children in that tiny flat on the second floor wasn't easy. Especially when I thought about the huge back yard we had plucked them from back in Portland.

Clyde worked full time at General Motors in the plant by night, and attended school full time by day. He would study in the afternoon, then go to work at the plant. Things were into a fairly good routine until the day before he was going to join the union when Clyde was laid off from General Motors.

There we were with four hungry children, no job, and the rent due. Tuition was paid through the semester, but it was time to exercise faith. I was starting to wait with anticipation. Clyde and I started praying that God would provide a new job and for our needs while we waited for the new job to develop.

There was a big annual school banquet that I knew we weren't going to be able to attend. *Everybody* was going to it; it was the major event of the Grand Rapids social season. I was so disappointed that I was going to miss getting all dressed up and having an actual date with my husband. But I pushed my thoughts aside and concentrated on the daily routine.

Then Clyde came home from school and said, "Look what was in my mail box!" It was tickets to the banquet! I was thrilled and excited. This was almost too good to be true.

Then I decided to pray a little selfishly. I asked God for a way that I'd be able to get my hair done for the banquet and just for good measure, I asked that I'd also be able to have a corsage.

A week before the banquet I didn't give up. I knew I could fix my own hair and I really didn't need flowers. But I kept on praying, with eager anticipation.

Then a postcard came in the mail. "Welcome to Grand Rapids. You're entitled to a free shampoo and wave at the Tracy Beauty Academy." God had answered my prayer! I was so thrilled and amazed at how He answered my prayer that I didn't dare continue to pray for flowers.

The day before the banquet, a brand new, stainless steel razor blade came with an advertising flyer in the mail. Oh boy! Clyde would have a clean shave for the banquet and I'd have my hair done. Clyde had even arranged to find a baby-sitter for nothing.

I was so excited to attend the banquet and it felt good to be all fixed up. I was wearing a favorite pink dress, with an iridescent layer of organdy. I felt so pretty with my hair done in the latest style. The banquet room was beautifully decorated, and the table centerpieces were bathed in candlelight. After Clyde told me how pretty I looked, it didn't matter that I didn't have a corsage for the evening.

Soon after we arrived, one of the young men came up to me with the biggest corsage I've ever seen. He explained to me, "Since last Sunday was Mother's Day, my Mom asked that I bring this corsage from Sunday and give it to a wife of one of the students."

I was stunned. The corsage was multicolored with white roses, baby's breath, and pink carnations, and it was so large I had to turn it sideways to be able to wear it. I'd never seen anything like it. It was the most beautiful corsage I've ever had, and it was the one that God supplied. It was that night that I started seeing how God delights in the small things in life.

The banquet was a wonderful night and the magic of the night stayed with me. It didn't take Clyde long to find a new job. God provided necessities, but there wasn't much money for anything extra. Clyde studied at home in the chaos of the children.

While I wasn't a registered student at the Bible college, I attended as many daily chapel services as I could. I also accompanied Clyde to as many classes I could. Tim was a preschooler at the time, so I'd pack him up and go to school. Little did we know that Tim would grow up to attend Bible college and be a pastor himself some day. The professors and students loved having a small child in class, and Tim loved to go. Some days they would ask him to sing. It was in these classes and the chapel services that I tried to learn how to be the best kind of a pastor's wife I could be.

Mr. Miles conducted different Bible studies. One day he said, "Gerrie, I'd like you to meet Bernice and Bill.

They're Arab Christians." My antennae went up, knowing the tension between the Arabs and the Jews. As much as I respected and admired Mr. Miles, I never pursued his invitation to meet them.

~

One day I went to a lady's elegant, elaborate coffee in a beautiful home in Grand Rapids. There were about thirty women there and I took a seat next to one of the most beautiful women I'd ever encountered. We began chatting, learning a bit about one another. When she realized I'd come more than one hundred miles to attend this occasion, she said, "I think I know who you are! Are you a friend of John Miles?"

I was surprised. "Yes! We're very close friends," I told her.

She laughed and grabbed my arm. "I'm Bernice Azkoul, the one he's been wanting you to meet!" She was Mr. Miles's Arabic friend. Bernice and I instantly became the closest of friends. She insisted I stay that night with them, and when I called Clyde he didn't see any reason why I shouldn't.

Bernice and I talked the night away and learned that we had far more in common than different, despite our heritage. Together we conspired that we would surprise Mr. Miles the next day during the chapel service.

Bernice drove to the Bible college and we walked into the rear of the chapel. When Mr. Miles looked up and saw us walking in arm-in-arm, he couldn't believe it. He stopped the music and said, "Students, I'd like you to witness this. This is a most unusual site. Today in our midst we have an Arab woman and Jewish woman arm-in-arm." His eyes held a twinkle and he grinned. Mr. Miles was so happy to see God had brought the two of us together.

Chapter 16

SETTLING IN

THINGS WERE GOOD at Bible college, but I missed having my own home. We improved our little flat slowly. When Mr. and Mrs. Miles purchased a new stove they gave us their old one, which was almost like brand new. This meant I didn't have to keep a chair propped up against the oven door anymore.

Mr. Johnson, the Sunday school superintendent at Calvary Church, kept asking me to teach Sunday school. I continued politely refusing. I had all I could handle with four children, Clyde working full time and going to school full time. But Mr. Johnson was persistent. He just kept patiently asking each week.

Then, on one hot and humid July evening, the kids were complaining about the heat. It was sweltering hot in that upstairs apartment with little ventilation. It had been so dry and we had not had rain in weeks. We were all trying to stay cool. I was talking to Mr. Johnson on the phone again about teaching Sunday school.

Beside me, my young daughter Lori was leaning into the night, looking through the window screen, her little nose pressed against it. She was trying desperately to cool off. Then, in the distance, we could hear thunder. Everyone was excited it was going to rain. I was chatting with Mr. Johnson on the phone when all of a sudden the screen broke and Lori started to lunge forward out the second-story window. Frantically I grabbed for her and snagged her by the foot as she dangled above the concrete twenty feet below. I gathered her back in the apartment, holding her tight and calming her fright. Our hearts were racing against each other in embrace.

Mr. Johnson had heard me scream when I dropped the phone. I collected my wits and in a shaken voice I picked up the phone.

"Mr. Johnson," I said with conviction, "I'd love to teach Sunday school." I felt God was trying to get my attention that day and it worked. I've been teaching Sunday school or Bible classes ever since.

Our neighborhood wasn't the best, but it wasn't the worst. Maybe two steps up from the worst. One night I heard a local radio broadcast announce that there had been a robbery and the police were looking for someone armed and dangerous in our neighborhood. I gathered the children and told them I wanted them to stay by me and I listened as a mother would for any unusual night noises. When we heard the footsteps on the back stairs, I also saw the shadow of a man crouching against the wall.

I picked up the longest knife I had and kept the children behind me. I was ready to stab him, if I had to protect my children. I could hear the commotion down below, from the police, and the next thing we heard were footsteps going downstairs and people yelling. I didn't go to the window, or the door. I just held onto the children, thankful we were safe. I listened for results the next day on the radio to learn that the robber had been captured.

While we were living in that little apartment, all four of our children really needed to go to the dentist. So, I made a dentist appointment for them. Two days before we needed to go, the dentist office called to inform me that because Clyde was a student, they would only see the children if I paid in cash.

We didn't have cash, but I told the dentist's bookkeeper, "Okay."

I hung up the phone and prayed, "Lord, I don't know how to pray for this, but we have to have fifty dollars." Two days later, I still didn't know how I was going to pay the dental bill, but it was time to go. My son Mike kept combing his curly hair, trying to make it straight. The children had all gotten into the spirit of the dental visit and were dressed up and ready to go. I was trying to tell them we weren't going to go after all when my friend Patsy called.

"Gerrie, we were at your house last night," Patsy said breathlessly. "You weren't there, but the door was unlocked, so we just went on in. There's something for you in the refrigerator." Vicky giggled and took a breath. "They call it cold cash," she continued. "My father said he'd woken up the night before and God was speaking to him to help out that young pastor."

I opened the refrigerator and I didn't see anything unusual. But when I explored a little deeper, I found fifty dollars tucked under an egg in an egg carton—exactly what we needed.

I packed the children into the car and drove off to the dentist. When I shared this story with Patsy, I don't know who was more in awe of seeing how God uses others to provide for us. Patsy and her husband Gordon have been our dear friends for many years.

Chapter 17

MONTGOMERY STREET

Y FAITH WAS really beginning to grow. I missed having a home more each day. I began praying to be able to find a house that would be affordable. So one day, just to humor me, Clyde took me house hunting. We found a house on Montgomery Street, and it was exactly what we wanted. It was almost like our old house in Kalamazoo before we had moved to Portland.

There were plenty of bedrooms for our large family, a dining room, a living room, and a nice small yard. I was thrilled at the thought of moving my children to their own backyard. Clyde and I prayed, "God, we want Your perfect will. If this is it, You can provide the way."
I called the realtor. His name was Mr. Albert and he took a liking to both of us right away. I liked him, too. He was Jewish and he and I seemed to click, especially when we discovered we shared the same birthday. When Mr. Albert found out who I was, he realized he knew who my father was. Mr. Albert suggested that Clyde and I simply borrow money from my father.

I smiled and quietly told him, "I can't really do that. We're strictly on our own."

Mr. Albert was very curious about my background, and how we ended up leaving the position we had in Portland to go to the ministry. He was so intrigued with our story that he made an appointment with Mr. Miles, the Bible college president, to talk to Mr. Miles about us. Mr. Miles was able to confirm that we were sincere.

Mr. Albert came by one day and said, "I'll tell you what. I'll pay the down payment, you play the closing costs."

I was shocked at his offer. But sadly, Clyde told him, "Mr. Albert, this is very generous, but we don't have the closing costs."

Mr. Albert's mouth dropped open in surprise. "Then what are you doing looking at houses?" he asked.

We were embarrassed. "I'm so sorry, Mr. Albert. We had no business even taking up your time. Clyde and I have no extra money," I explained. "I guess I was just dreaming."

Mr. Albert was completely baffled. He wasn't angry or annoyed. He simply replied, "I'll think of something. We have to find a way to get you kids into this house."

So Clyde and I dropped the idea. We had prayed, "God if You want us there, You have a reason for putting us there and You'll get us there." If God wasn't going to provide for us to move to Montgomery Street, then we'd remain happy in our little apartment. We simply dismissed the thought. But then, a few days later, Mr. Albert dropped by the apartment and said, "All right kids, I'll pay the down payment and the closing costs."

I was stunned. "Mr. Albert! You are wonderful!"

Mr. Albert didn't seem to even hear my comment. He went on to say, "You'll have to tell the bank it's a gift from your father. It's not legal for me to pay your costs, but you can accept a gift from a family member. So that's all you have to do."

Clyde and I looked at each other. I knew what Clyde would say before he said it. "I can't lie, Mr. Albert," Clyde responded.

I nodded, "As much as I want that house, Clyde and I cannot lie to the bank."

"Don't be ridiculous!" Mr. Albert said. "I've made an appointment for you on Friday at eleven o'clock. Here's the address." And he walked out.

Clyde and I decided to keep the appointment at the bank with Mr. Albert. I remember that there was an enormous, long flight of marble steps to walk up to the bank front door. As Clyde and I started walking up those stairs, we started to giggle and finally were laughing knowing that the deal would explode when they asked us where the money was coming for the down payment and closing costs. But both Clyde and I had agreed that we would not lie about it. It was a gift, but not from my father, it was a gift from Mr. Albert.

But God had a plan.

The banker was a kind, soft-spoken, Christian man and appreciated our honesty. He looked over all the paperwork, our credit history, and our current financial situation carefully. He made some notes on a legal pad, then put his pen down and leaned back into his chair. "Let's see what we can work out," he said to Mr. Albert as he took off his glasses.

"How much are you willing to pay Mrs. Mills for painting the trim on that house?" the kindly banker asked Mr. Albert. I looked at Clyde and wondered what the banker was talking about. I was not a house painter! Mr. Albert let out a giant belly laugh. And then I let out a big breath that I seemed to have been holding since we first sat down. I suddenly realized that it was all going to work out. The bank allowed Mr. Albert to pay the down payment and closing costs as a labor exchange to upgrade the Montgomery Street house to bank specifications.

Mr. Albert was so excited that he actually went to the hardware store and bought cans and cans of paint! He brought paint for the trim on the outside of the house as promised, but also cans of paint for the inside to paint the kitchen and to antique the cupboards—and all because God had further plans for us in that house.

~

When we moved into the house on Montgomery Street it was a grand day. Clyde and I prayed, "Lord we want to be placed in the exact home You have for us, where people in that neighborhood need You. If there are neighbors that need to know about Jesus, please give us the opportunity to share Him."

The very first neighbor I met was Mary Woodward, a little Italian girl who lived next door. She was full of fun, with a vivacious personality. I liked her instantly and we developed a warm friendship. Eventually Mary opened her tender heart toward God and wanted to know how she too could have eternal life. She accepted Jesus and just like me she couldn't keep it to herself. She was so happy to know she had eternal life and had peace that she shared it with her neighbor, Carol Loomis.

Carol and Mary went to church together and afterward they'd gather on my front porch or in the dining room and talk for hours and hours. I would try to answer all their questions, and Carol came to know the Lord, too.

Carol was so concerned about her husband Dave; he had been belligerent with Carol about not going to church. One day, Dave dropped by while I was playing a song on the record player. The song sparked some dialogue between Dave and me, and he began to open up.

A dialogue opened between us and as David realized the need for Jesus in his life, he decided that day to get serious about his relationship with God. David made a decision to accept the Lord in his life, just two weeks after his wife had.

One by one, neighbors up and down Montgomery Street became Christians. All of us were excited together to see how God was working.

Jan was the most interesting character on Montgomery Street. She was tall and muscular with wild, frizzy brown hair. She was a cook in a restaurant. Jan was the roughest, toughest woman I had ever encountered and I was honestly afraid of her. I avoided her every week, watching her fight with the man next door. It bothered me so much, that I'd run back into the house when I heard the quarreling erupt. Jan's fighting disrupted the whole neighborhood, and everyone would retreat into their homes and close their doors, fearing what could happen. There was such hate between Jan and her neighbor.

Jan and her husband, Kyle, lived kitty-corner across the street from me. I stayed as far away from their house as I could. One day my children were playing outside and their ball rolled across the street. This day, I had no choice but to go over to Jan's house. I had to go get the ball.

I walked over there very slowly and when I arrived, Jan's husband Kyle had already picked up the ball. After he handed it to me I thanked him and we struck up an innocent conversation.

"I understand your husband is studying to be a minister," Kyle said.

"Yes he is," I nodded, trying to get away quickly. I walked back home with ball.

But the next time I saw Kyle, he waved and I waved back. We developed a nodding acquaintance and I began to notice things like he was home in the evenings and his wife wasn't.

On one of those hot summer Michigan nights I looked out and saw Kyle sitting outside on the front porch steps. He waved and called, "Hello, there!"

I smiled and waved back, but I didn't do much more than that. Deep down I was afraid of the whole situation over there. Kyle was chatting with Mary, my next-door neighbor, one day and somehow I got involved in the conversation. One thing led to another and Kyle revealed that he used to go to church. He went on to confess that he'd made a terrible mistake by getting very drunk one night, took this woman out, she got pregnant, and he married her. This woman was Jan.

It was so sad. I really felt sorry for Kyle, for they were so mismatched. He had a sweet side and there was nothing sweet about Jan. She was an angry, bitter, scary woman!

One evening Kyle walked over to our front porch and sat down on the steps. He told me that he thought that God could never forgive him for all the mistakes he'd made. I assured him that God could forgive him and showed him how in Psalm 51 where God forgave David. Tears filled Kyle's eyes in hope.

I told him, "Let's pray together and ask God to create within you a clean heart and that you're sorry for what you've done."

Kyle prayed with me, and God did create within him a clean heart. He could hardly wait for Sunday. Clyde encouraged him to go to a church of his choice that preached the Bible and the first time Kyle went, he returned with excitement and so much joy and fulfillment. He could remember every word the pastor spoke that day and spent hours talking with Clyde about it.

The following Sunday Kyle was getting ready to leave for church when Jan walked out, demanding that he stay home. As Kyle backed the car out of their driveway, Jan stood behind the car, widened her stance, put her hand up, and said, "You aren't going anywhere, mister."

Kyle put the car in park, got out, and walked to the back of his car. Calmly he said, "Jan, step aside, I'm going to church."

Jan glowered at him, "No you're not! Park that car and get back inside."

Nobody fought with Jan. And truthfully, Kyle was afraid of her. So Kyle got back into the car, pulled it back into the driveway, and stopped going to church, avoiding another fight.

Kyle became very sad. He'd had such hopes that he was going to have a happier life. He had felt the joy and freedom of being a saved Christian and did not want a life without it. As a result, Kyle became very discouraged and despondent.

One day when I was visiting the Bible college, Mr. Miles said, "Gerrie, you look like you've got something on your mind."

I told him about Kyle being discouraged, and about Kyle's tough, mean-spirited wife that nobody would ever be able to reach.

Mr. Miles offered interesting advice, "You know, Gerrie, maybe you need to be more like what she is, so she will be more comfortable with you." I thought about Jan and her angry countenance, and her stained cook's uniform pinned together with safety pins. I didn't think there was anyone more opposite me on the whole planet.

I looked at Mr. Miles curiously, "You mean, like, tough?" I asked.

He laughed, "Yes! Like 'tough'," he confirmed.

So I got tough. I went home, took off my stylish clothes, put on a pair of jeans and rolled them up, and went outside looking for Jan. I found her out in her yard, and struck up a conversation with her. In my "toughest" nasally voice, laced with my Chicago accent, I said, "Jan, you've got to come to my Bible study some time."

Jan didn't even look up from the flowerbed. "I don't do Bible studies," she growled. "I don't need any of that. Just like I told Kyle. It's not going to be in our life. That church stuff is not a part of us."

Boldly I nasalled, "Kyle misses going to church. He seemed to enjoy it."

Jan continued to dig in the dirt, "That's just too bad. That's the way it's going to be around my house."

That was "tough day number one." Then there was "tough day number two," with kind of the same thing, me downgrading my fashion style, putting on my toughest swagger, and sauntering out the front door.

Eventually, Jan agreed to come just to see what it was all about. I was thrilled. She came to church with her white cook's uniform stained, pinned together, equally stained white shoes, and white bobby socks. By this time many of my church friends had also been praying for Jan and they were very warm and hospitable toward her.

One day I decided to really start getting tough. Dressed in my "tough look" I went out about 11 a.m. and found Jan was again in the yard working in the dirt. I noticed that nothing seemed to grow in her flowerbeds, but she just liked to putter in the dirt.

"How's your old man, Jan?" I called in a raspy, hoarse voice, trying my best to sound tough.

"Not half bad," she replied. "How about yours?"

I put my palms toward the sky, "Eh, he's all right." I answered putting my hands on my hips.

I continued, "Jan, we gotta talk. We gotta start talking about a verse in the Bible."

Jan looked up. "Don't start preaching to me, woman," she cautioned.

I locked my knees in place and with a boldness I said, "I'm *gonna* talk to you." I was petrified, but I felt that day was the day to reach Jan.

Clyde and I were always partners in our neighborhood evangelism, and he knew that I had been trying desperately for a way to reach Jan. But I had forgotten to tell Clyde about my "tough" approach. Just as I was daring Jan to keep me from talking to her about that Bible verse, Clyde drove around the corner coming home for lunch. I thought to myself, "Oh no, what do I do now? I can't not be 'tough', but what will Clyde think if he sees me like this?" Then I decided

I'd just have fun with it. Jan and I were both standing at the curb when Clyde pulled up, rolled down the car window, and said, "Hi! How about some lunch?"

It was my first and only time that I ever did anything like this, but almost ignoring Clyde I tossed over my shoulder, in the toughest sounding voice I could muster, "Fix it yourself, big boy."

Clyde's brown eyes widened, his head snapped back a bit, and he asked, "What did you say?"

I made a sour face at Jan and then turned to Clyde in disgust, "You heard me, fix it yourself." I could see Clyde's reaction, he was getting mad. He left us at the curb and drove the car into our driveway.

Jan said admirably, "Way to go, there, Gerrie. That's telling him!"

I looked up at our house. I could see Clyde looking at me through the glass front door and I could tell he was angry. But I felt like this was a critical moment with Jan and at that instant, there was nothing I could do about Clyde. I turned to Jan in earnest and said, "Listen Jan, you gotta go home and start reading Kyle's Bible. It's time you got things right with God."

Jan frowned, "You heard me tell you not to preach to me!"

I widened my stance, the same way I'd seen Jan do behind Kyle's car, and I said, "I've only just begun."

Jan turned and walked away from me.

I sighed and ran up the walk into my house. With no explanation for the incredibly rude way I'd spoken to Clyde outside, I just said, (in my normal voice) "Clyde! We have to pray for Jan!"

Clyde was seething with anger and hurt at how I'd treated him. "You go ahead and pray" he answered. I tried to explain that I'd been playing tough with Jan and that I was making headway in reaching her heart. But that didn't impress Clyde. He was angry. Our argument was interrupted when the phone rang. Clyde answered and surprisingly it was Jan. She was so mad at me, and wanted Clyde to know it.

Clyde listened to her ranting about all the things that were wrong with me and then Clyde suggested some Bibles verses for Jan to read. He told her how to look them up in Kyle's Bible.

Clyde hung up the phone, realizing that maybe something was happening with Jan as a result of my toughness. As we started to discuss it, the phone rang again and it was Jan. She'd begun reading the verses Clyde had suggested and shouted, "Boy does this fit the man next door!"

Clyde said, "Jan, you want to read what speaks to you. I'm asking you to read Romans 10:9–10 seven times and let me know what you think about it: 'That if you confess with your mouth, "Jesus is Lord," and believe in your heart that God raised Him from the dead, you will be saved. For it is with your heart that you believe and are justified, and it is with your mouth that you confess and are saved'" (author's paraphrase).

Clyde hung up the phone and he and I began to pray for Jan. We were interrupted again by the phone ringing. It was Jan crying on the other end. She couldn't even talk, she was crying so hard.

We both ran out the front door and across the street. She was waiting at the door for us, with tears streaming down her cheeks. She informed us that she had called upon the

Lord for salvation and had asked Him to forgive her of her sins. Jan had questions and wanted to know more about the Gospel.

I said, "Jan, this is wonderful! We've got to tell Kyle when he comes home."

Jan wiped her eyes, "I can't." she sniffed. "I'm too scared."

I thought, "Jan? Scared?" I never knew she had a frightened bone in her body. Her two twin boys didn't know what to think when they saw their mother crying. They had never seen her cry before.

After lunch, Clyde went back to school, but I stayed with Jan keeping an eye out for Kyle. When Kyle came home, I ran outside and called, "Kyle, somebody else came to know the Lord today."

Kyle came up the walk and asked, "Which neighbor was it?" So many of the neighbors had become Christians and they were so excited for each other. Kyle loved to hear about this kind of news.

I replied, "Somebody near and dear to you."

"Who could that be?" Kyle asked.

I said, "Look around," as I turned my head toward Kyle's house. There was Jan in the doorway between the living room and dining room with a tear-stained face. Kyle stared at her in disbelief. "Jan? Was it you?" he asked.

Jan nodded, "Yep, it's me," she admitted. They hugged and hugged and cried together and it was the beginning of an entire new relationship between them.

One thing that still amuses me when I think about it happened the next day. Jan had been digging into the Word since her salvation the day before, when she called me slightly exasperated and asked, "I prayed the Sinner's Prayer, and then you told me to read the Book of John—but I found four of them! Which one did you want me to read?"

Later that week, I asked Jan if she'd like to go with me to the midweek service at our church. As the song leader started leading the music, all of a sudden Jan's hand shot up and she yelled out, "I want to sing that song they sing at Easter called 'He Lives'!"

The music director was a bit taken aback, but he said, "We'll be glad to do that. We've had a request for 'He Lives.'"

Afterward a lady from our church came up and introduced herself. "Hello, I'm Helen. You must be Jan." Jan frowned, "How can you tell, by my bobby socks?" Helen smiled, "No, because you have a new-Christian smile, and Gerrie said her neighbor had just come to know Jesus." Helen became Jan's mentor and dearest friend.

Jan and Kyle became involved in a local church, and Jan began cooking for the church affairs. Kyle did whatever he could to help and their two little twin boys entered Sunday school. After Clyde and I were called to our first church, I can remember walking down the aisle to greet the people and a big arm grabbed me and pulled me in. It was Jan. She and Kyle had driven down to surprise us.

Later in life, Kyle developed Alzheimer's disease. Jan chose to care for Kyle at home. She confided to me, "I made the first years of our marriage so miserable that I want to do everything I can, as long as I can, for him now." Clyde called on Kyle in Kyle's last months. Clyde asked him, "How do we get to heaven?" Even in Kyle's final stages of Alzheimer's, he looked at Clyde and said, "Jesus."

⌒

Our home was always open to the neighborhood or to anyone who needed a place to stay. At Thanksgiving time we had invited students over that were too far from home for the holiday. But we had one major challenge—we didn't have any money to buy all the groceries for the traditional meal.

It was faith time. Clyde and I prayed and asked God to supply our needs when a friend of ours, Bernie Schipper, called Clyde and asked, "Any way you'd like a turkey? I just won one at a big basketball game and we don't like turkey at our house." The next thing we knew there was a twenty-five-pound turkey showing up for Thanksgiving dinner. Somehow we came up with everything else to make a traditional meal.

The following year, it was prayer time again at Thanksgiving. It was getting to be fun to see how God would supply our needs. I wanted to invite all the students who couldn't be with family on the holiday again. But on our limited budget, it was impossible. Then, Thelma, one of the women I went to Bible study with, came up to me. "Gerrie, my family is going out of town for Thanksgiving. We'd like to help you with your Thanksgiving so we'd like buy your turkey and the trimmings this year." Two years in a row, God provided the essentials so that Clyde and I were able to host a wonderful Thanksgiving feast for our fellow students and their families.

I recall one Christmas when after purchasing small gifts for each of the children, there was no money for a Christmas tree. So I set out to find the best deal that I could on a small tree. I located a very nice tree with a price of ten dollars. For Clyde and me at that time in our lives, ten dollars might have well been one thousand! But I loved this beautiful tree and just prayed, as a Jewish girl who had missed many Christmas trees growing up, that the Lord would provide one for my children. I started talking to the tree lot attendant, explaining that my husband was a student at the Bible college. I kept talking and talking until he finally agreed to sell me the tree for one dollar!

Clyde was in his final year of Bible college when Mr. Miles asked Clyde if he'd be interested in preaching in Wellston, located on a lake in Northern Michigan. Clyde would have to drive the one hundred miles back and forth to remain in school. The church was an old historic church and keeping with the integrity of the historical period, it didn't even have a bathroom. I recall that when Clyde took our son Tim to the outhouse, Tim told him, "It stinks like a horse in here!"

It was our first taste of ministry and pastoring. We learned a valuable lesson there. One Sunday morning, Clyde and I had a terrible argument on the way to church. Clyde could hardly preach and I couldn't tell you one thing he said. After that we vowed that we would never ever allow ourselves to argue again on Sunday morning.

After graduation, this congregation gave us a call to stay there, but after careful consideration Clyde and I knew God had a different plan for us.

Grandma and Grandpa

My family when I was little

Bedonna (l.) and I

Clyde and I at his parents'
fiftieth anniversary, 1961

Daddy's postcard to
Clyde and me

Our family in 1966, while
Clyde was in Bible college

Our family in 1974

Moving to gold country

Clyde and I with
our "preacher's kids"

Pastor of the Year

Handing out Bibles
in Russia

Our whole family

With John Hagee

Clyde and Gerrie

Chapter 18

THE PARSON OF
QUINCY, MICHIGAN

S CLYDE APPROACHED graduation from Bible college
we still didn't know what we were going to do. Where
would God have us serve? Others knew they would
be missionaries or pastors. But there were a few of us that
weren't sure. We just had to keep praying that God would
show us His perfect will. Clyde had confidence as a businessman, but not as a pastor and silently we were scared to
death.

As we were praying about where God would send us,
different speaking engagements would come in. When Clyde
and I went to one of the first ones that invited him, it was to
what was definitely the most rural church I've ever encountered. It was deep in a farming community, with hard-working
men and women who came to church directly from their
farms. It was common to find manure on the men's boots. I
was as out of place as I could be with the stench of manure
permeating the sanctuary. This tiny church was made up of
about fifteen people and they found me a bit curious, too.
They were looking at me like I'd dropped from outer space.

Clyde said, "Gerrie, this might be pretty good for our first
church." I gasped. "Clyde, you've got to be kidding!"

There were other places we investigated but nothing gave us the solid pull from the Lord. And then we went to speak in Quincy, Michigan, a rural community about eighty miles from Kalamazoo. Both Clyde and I found that the church in Quincy complimented our personalities. The people were friendly, interested in our family as well as Clyde's pastoring abilities. During our visit, a big snowstorm blew in that closed highways and made it impossible for us to travel back home.

Clyde and I stayed overnight with church members through the storm. When we finally got home, Clyde discovered that he had left his Bible there. When the church board extended a call to Clyde to come and serve as their pastor, Clyde felt a very strong leading, because he had never, ever left his Bible behind before.

At that point a faculty member of the college said to Clyde, "I want you to make sure this is really God's will because this congregation has a history of not being good to their pastors." Despite that warning, Clyde and I continued to pray and felt God directing us to answer this call to serve at Quincy. We found out that everything the president warned us of was true within the first few months we were there.

It was a bitter cold January when Clyde and I moved our children into a lovely ranch style home with four bedrooms in Quincy. The house was a "parsonage," a home for the pastor that belonged to the church. After an exhausting day of unpacking, I can remember looking out the big living room window and seeing a farmer on his tractor driving across the field on the other side of the road.

"Look Clyde!" Knowing nothing about farming, I exclaimed in wonder. "He's plowing the field!" Clyde laughed very hard. Remember, it was January, when no plowing can take place in the Midwest. The farmer was spreading manure on his field with a manure spreader. There was a reason they called me "Mrs. Green Acres" those first few months in Quincy.

The only time I'd ever been in the country was traveling from one city to the other. Now this was my new home. I was willing to try to adapt to the country lifestyle, but I'm afraid my platinum blonde hair, high style fashion sense, and "city ways" were a bit of shock to the people of Quincy.

Even though we felt lead by God to serve in Quincy, it still took a long time to adjust to the new job, lifestyle, community, and culture. In the beginning of our life at Quincy, we drove to Grand Rapids almost every week because we missed everyone back there so much. Ministry was entirely new to us and people seemed to take advantage of our naiveté.

I recall that one of the women in our congregation offered Clyde fresh meat from the butcher, if he'd help her carry it all home. "Oh, I have meat to give you, if you'll carry all the beef from the butcher shop and put it in my freezer," she boasted. Clyde eagerly helped her, knowing that home grown beef would be a wonderful treat for our family.

Clyde was so proud to bring home a large package of what he thought was prime steaks or a big roast. I'll never forget opening that package of meat, wrapped in the white waxy butcher paper. She'd sent Clyde home with the cow's liver!

Another time, shortly after that, a couple in the church invited us to share in their farm products. It turned out that they wanted help killing some chickens! Clyde had his first butchering experience of chopping the heads off chickens. Again packages of meat, wrapped in butcher's paper were sent home, with the toughest hens ever grown for our family to try to eat.

But those first experiences as a new pastor in a farming community turned out to be mild compared to what lay ahead. Within a month or two, a couple of older ladies in the church decided they were going to run the church. Clyde and I found ourselves in a precarious position of redirecting their leadership. We had our hands full with them.

Clyde had to inform them that they weren't going to be in that place of leadership. There was a big fuss, with threats of leaving, but Clyde held firm. Their style of leadership was not in concert with how Clyde would pastor. In a fury, they left the church. This was difficult, because the church was very small at the time. With Clyde and me, and our four children, we probably only had about thirty-four members. It was not good for people to leave the church. But Clyde was confident that this was something that had to be addressed and we soon realized God allowed that to happen because He was ready to give us a big increase. We may have lost a few, but it opened the doors to many more in the months to come.

When I look back to what we went through that first year in Quincy, I was shocked at how the community thought they had a right to an opinion about many things I did. I can remember we were there about six months, and we had a stretch of very hot weather. I was hanging clothes out on the clothesline in the backyard, wearing Bermuda shorts. Then I ran to the grocery, grabbed a few items, and came back home.

Within a few minutes someone knocked on the door. When I answered, there were three women who had become a self-appointed committee, informing me that they wanted to talk to me and tell me how inappropriate it was that I was wearing Bermuda shorts, trying to attract the men.

We lived way out in the country with a dirt road on each side of the house. Never in my wildest dreams did I ever think that wearing Bermuda shorts was improper, or that I was trying to attract men. But what was more baffling was that these women thought they had a right to admonish me.

I wanted to quit on the spot. After they left, I cried with my heart broken in two. I was trying to be a good pastor's wife and a good mother to my children. It was clear to me that as hard as I was trying to fit into their community and culture, nothing I did would please them.

Clyde assured me that he would leave it if was necessary. He confirmed that he was pleased with my work as a pastor's wife and with my ministry. He told me he was proud of my attempts to fit in the Quincy community; his kind encouragement made me want to call upon the Lord for help. By this time both of us were sick of all the bickering and backbiting within the congregation.

I opened up my Bible and prayed, "God, I just need You to really reveal to me what to do." He showed me the verses in Hebrews 10:35—36, "So do not throw away this confident trust in the Lord. Remember the great reward it brings you! Patient endurance is what you need now, so that you will continue to do God's will. Then you will receive all that he has promised."

God comforted my heart and soul and gave me a strength and determination to pursue His perfect plan for us. Clyde and I knew that He had called us to Quincy and we would remain faithful until He showed us it was time to leave.

I hung in there, and by Thanksgiving I was starting to think things might work out in Quincy. During Christmastime, I was coordinating a children's Christmas service. I selected Pete, an adorable first grader, to play the part of the little drummer boy. Evelyn, one of the women who had been criticizing me at every opportunity, came up to me and demanded that someone else play the drummer boy. Evelyn was part of the self-appointed committee and she was trying very hard to support the other two members. Evelyn wanted their approval and was willing to do just about anything to gain it.

When I didn't immediately cave into her demands, she picked up a pencil and pushed the pencil lead into my chin, leaned forward, and glared at me eye to eye. She turned the pencil point into my chin and said, "The drummer boy is not going to be Pete."

I glared right back and said, "Yes. It will be played by Pete."

With a cold, hard stare she turned the pencil point again into my chin and said, "No, it won't."

I'm no coward. I just stood there, daring her to actually hurt me with this pencil in front of the church. I said, "The drummer boy will be played by Pete." She twisted the pencil again. "No. It will be played by..." and she finished the sentence with her friend's son's name.

What was happening? I had tried so hard to be a good witness and friend to this woman and not return her bitterness and spite each time she tossed it my way. I backed down and gave in. I conceded that the other boy would play the little drummer boy. I went home defeated and forlorn. How was this going to be a happy Christmas with that kind of attitude and atmosphere right in our church?

But I didn't give up. I was determined to make the church as enjoyable as I could. As new people started coming in it was easier to forget or put behind some of the difficult circumstances. And remarkably, Evelyn became my dearest friend and staunchest supporter. Her children were the same ages as mine, and they were in and out of each other's houses all day long. Whenever my children were hungry, they would head to Evelyn's house because she had the best baked goods, the Schwan's ice cream, and the best Sloppy Joes. As I learned more about Evelyn's background, I came to understand that her initial hurtful reactions to me were a result of her abusive past.

Today Evelyn and I share forty years of a close relationship and I count her as one of my closest and dearest friends. Evelyn doesn't even remember much about the bad parts of our first few years together, other than that she thought I was a little "city slicker" when I arrived in Quincy. What she does remember are the twenty other years we worked side-by-side together in love and friendship serving God, and the twenty years since then that we have remained such dear friends.

Clyde's sister Mae and her husband John had noticed that Clyde was putting a lot of money into our old car. Since I was doing a lot of speaking around the region, they were concerned about it breaking down far from home. To support our budding ministry in Quincy, Mae and John contacted all Clyde's sisters and brothers, and together they bought a brand new Chevrolet for us to drive.

After that car wore out, our church members saw the need for safe transportation for the pastor and his family. One

Sunday I walked into the service to find Mother and Daddy sitting in a back pew. They had been invited to be present when our church surprised us with a second new car.

One of my favorite memories of how God brought new people into the church at Quincy happened on a rainy afternoon. Our little country church desperately needed a pianist. The pianist we had played by ear, but had no formal training. She did the best she could, but services were not really enhanced with her music.

One day Clyde was walking along the country road to our house when a car pulled up. A beautiful young woman rolled down her window and asked, "What a lovely church! Are you by any chance the pastor?"

Clyde told her yes, he was indeed the pastor. She introduced herself as Sue Stout, she was moving to the Quincy area, and was looking for a new church home. Her parents were with her, and they had been driving around her new area that day, anticipating a transfer for her husband to our community.

Clyde chatted with her briefly, learning that her husband was an Indiana State Trooper. Sue asked, "What time is your service on Sunday?" Clyde told her and invited her to join us. "OK, my husband and I will probably see you Sunday," she answered.

"I'll be looking for you, Sue," Clyde told her. "You mentioned your husband works as a State Trooper, what do you do?" Before Sue could answer, her father piped up, "She's a pianist. The most talented one in the state!"

Sue and her husband Alan showed up that next Sunday and every Sunday thereafter for the next twenty years. And Sue's father's boasting had been correct. Something magical happened when Sue played the piano. Our congregation's music turned around when Sue played. Her talent was extraordinary and she jumped in with creative energy, inspired by God. Sue developed all the children's music ministries, the choir music, and became my dearest friend.

While those early years in Quincy involved turmoil within church, all our children except Mike enjoyed the new rural lifestyle immediately. But before long, Mike loved it, too. But it was still an unsettling time for me. I wasn't able to relax in my role as pastor's wife, and often I felt my ministry within the church was resented or even thwarted. I was so uncomfortable at the loss of my privacy. My neighbor would actually listen in on our party-line telephone conversations.

Clyde and I were contemplating resigning the church at Quincy and going to work with Campus Crusade for Christ. A friend had paid for us to attend a conference with Campus Crusade. There we prayed about moving to California. We didn't know it, but our children were all praying for us to move to California, too. They had visions of surfing, Disneyland, and worshiping with Hollywood celebrities. Clyde and I fell in love with Campus Crusade. They taught us how to share our faith, and as Clyde and I began sharing it back in Quincy, one-by-one people started to know Jesus.

But as God would have it, we did not move to California. It would require too many days away from the children each month and God directed us to remain in Quincy for the next twenty years.

One of the friends I loved to look back and remember was my daughter Lori's Brownie leader, Virginia. Lori loved this Brownie leader and every night without fail, Lori would pray for Virginia to come to know Jesus. Virginia was one of the loveliest women in the community.

After I came back from Campus Crusade in California, I was eager to practice sharing the Four Spiritual Laws that I'd learned at their conference. So I called Virginia and said, "Virginia let's get together. I just learned something new at my conference, and I need to practice. Can I share something with you?"

I met Virginia at her house, where I shared the Four Spiritual Laws with her. I explained that God loved her and had a wonderful plan for her life. I went on to tell her how she could experience this wonderful plan. I shared with Virginia that each of us must individually receive Jesus Christ as Savior and Lord. That's how we can know and experience God's love and plan for our lives.

I told Virginia how she could ask Jesus to come into her life. I gave her a simple prayer:

> *Dear Jesus,*
> *I need You in my life. I am so grateful that You died on the cross for my sins. I invite You to come into my life as my Lord and Savior. Thank You for forgiving me of my sins and for granting me eternal life with You in heaven. Take control of all the areas in my life and help me to be the kind of person You want me to be.*
> *Amen.*

I'll never forget what Virginia told me later. She said that I wasn't even out of the driveway when she went into the bathroom, locked the door, and got down on her knees and prayed that prayer, inviting Jesus into her life.

The next week when I picked up Lori, I waved at Virginia and I knew immediately that she was a new Christian. She had the glow.

I said, "Virginia, I can tell, I can tell!" She started laughing. "You can tell?" I nodded gleefully, "That's right. You prayed to receive Jesus, didn't' you?" She hugged me and said, "I did and what a difference it's making in my life."

We got together the next day. Virginia told me that she had been in a depression, but you'd never know it to look at her. A doctor had prescribed a relaxing vacation, somewhere she'd always wanted to go. So her husband John had taken Virginia to Hawaii where they stayed in a beautiful hotel with a fabulous ocean view.

"Are you happy, now?" John had asked Virginia.

Sadly, Virginia had answered John, "No, that emptiness is still there." John was very concerned and upset that he couldn't bring his wife happiness. When Virginia returned from her vacation and continued her depression, her doctor suggested she redecorate her kitchen. Virginia had a flair for interior decorating. She completed the kitchen only to have this depression worsen.

"The day that I asked Jesus into my life, I gained a whole new attitude and a whole new purpose," Virginia explained to me. "I feel like my life is just beginning." Virginia asked God, "Lord, what will You have me do with my life?"

She began teaching Sunday school and all these years later, she's still working with children. Eventually, Virginia's entire family came to the Lord. Lori was excited to see the change in Virginia's countenance. As young as she was, Lori recognized that the power of her prayers had sparked Virginia's heart.

~

I was on a speaking tour at a Bible conference at Winnona Lake, Indiana. While I was sitting on the platform with the other speakers, I saw the most elegant, stately woman sitting in the audience. She was a tall, black lady dressed in a native African garb. She struck me as someone of royal heritage, for she had such grace, and the movements of a queen. I leaned over to one of the other speakers and asked, "Who is that woman?"

"That's Marta," my colleague answered. "Marta Gabre–Tsadick." I said, "She's beautiful!" My friend nodded in agreement. "You should hear her story," she told me.

I was intrigued. That night I was informed that Marta would be speaking about her escape from Ethiopia. I heard that it had only been three weeks since she had come to the United States. What would Marta have to say?

The room where Marta was scheduled to speak was extremely crowded when I arrived, but I was able to get a spot in the corner where I sat down expectantly. Marta began talking about her life in Ethiopia. She was a political icon because Marta was the first woman senator in Ethiopia, and had served as Ethiopia's first lady when Emperor Haile Selassie's wife passed away.

Marta explained that when the communists took over Ethiopia, it didn't matter what your title was, they killed anyone who had influence in the government. Just hours before Marta was to be assassinated, she and her husband and children were able to escape the politically ravaged country.

Marta shared the story of her escape, detailing one miracle after another. The entire audience was spellbound. Everyone in the room was touched by Marta's story and shocked by the brutality and tragedy of her life. Our mouths were agape as Marta talked about not being able to tell her parents or servants where she was going because they would have been beaten. She couldn't kiss the doorpost when she left. She told the story of her miraculous escape and how God protected her and her family as they fled to safety in Kenya.

I sat there in tears until there was nothing left in me to cry. Somehow I found a telephone and called Clyde. Through my sobs, I told Clyde, "I just heard the most remarkable story I've ever heard!" Clyde's reaction surprised me, "How do you know what she's saying is true?" he asked me doubtfully. "We can't just bring anyone in to our church to talk, Gerrie."

I wasn't giving up. "I know her story is true, Clyde," I said.

"Gerrie," Clyde asked, "how can you know after just listening to her talk?"

"I just know it!" I told him.

I was becoming exasperated at Clyde's doubting spirit and lack of compassion. "We've got to have her come!" I exclaimed. "Before long she'll be so well-known we won't be able to get her!"

I could imagine Clyde shaking his head, "I don't know. We have to look into it, find out more about her," he told me regretfully.

I was so upset with Clyde when I hung up the phone. I took a deep breath, held it a minute, and then let it out in one long courage-gathering sigh. I pulled myself together and called Clyde back.

"Clyde, you don't understand," I implored. "There's not a woman here who will ever be the same because of Marta's story."

But Clyde wasn't budging. "I don't think so, Gerrie. Not until we've checked her out more thoroughly."

I hung up the second time, more determined than ever to bring Marta to our congregation. So I asked myself, "What can I do?" I knew the folks back home would love Marta and be inspired by her story. So I decided to do something I'd never done before. I went over Clyde's head.

I placed a third phone call to Mac, the chairman of our church board. I was emphatic, "Mac, I've just heard the most amazing woman speak of her escape from Ethiopia. I want to bring her to our church, but when I talked with Clyde he didn't seem to understand the quality of this woman." I stopped for a breath. "Mac, she is extraordinary and will make a huge impact on our congregation."

Mac paused a bit and then said, "I'll take full responsibility; get her lined up to come." And so I did.

Clyde was annoyed, but he wasn't angry and when he saw my enthusiasm, he knew Marta had to be something out of the ordinary. We brought her to our church to speak and by the time Marta was finished, Clyde's suit had two shades of gray because one shade was from his tears. Clyde apologized to Marta over and over that he had doubted the validity of her story, and we became her biggest supporters from that time on.

Marta wrote a book about her escape and we had the dedication at our church. She and her husband Demeke Tekle-Wold went on to establish Project Mercy, a Christian non-profit organization in Yetebon, Ethiopia. Over the past eleven years, Project Mercy's original mission has been expanded to include community development and self-help programs.

I took Marta to Maranatha Writer's Conference with me. I was hoping she would share her story with others there. But Marta was reluctant to speak because she didn't trust anybody since there were so many spies for the Ethiopian communist government. When *Moody Monthly* and *The 700 Club* wanted to interview Marta, she refused. She was too frightened. But when people heard her story they wanted to be a part of her ministry. Eventually I was able to persuade Marta that by telling her story to the media, she could garner more support for her mission, so she agreed to the interviews.

That was the beginning of a whole new career for Marta. She was featured in all the Christian magazines and television shows and told her story to millions. Eventually Marta and Deme appeared on the cover of *Life* magazine.

Marta and I became soul mates. Our kids loved Marta, but got upset with me because I would compare their manners to the beautiful manners Marta's children had. Marta's children spoke quietly and said, "Yes ma'am" and "No sir," and even bowed in respect. My children complained, "You want us to be just like them!"

Marta and Deme remain close, dear friends of ours. Clyde and I and our children have supported Marta's mission for more than thirty years.

Chapter 19

IKE AND THE
INDY 500

I T WAS THE late sixties, with the country rattled politically. In our little conservative community, most of the upheaval was experienced watching the nightly news. But one day, Clyde received a call from one of the doctors in our town.

"Clyde, I've got some interesting people to send out to your church," he told Clyde with a great deal of concern in his voice. Clyde knew this doctor was an active member at another church in town, so he asked him, "Why not take them to your church? The doctor sighed, "I don't think they would be accepted at my church."

Clyde was curious, "What do you mean by that?" The doctor paused and then told Clyde, "They're hippies. With long, long hair, and running around barefoot." The doctor continued, "There was an altercation with the law and one just blew smoke in the sheriff's face. No one in authority knows what to do with these people. We thought maybe you could help."

Clyde said, "Send them along. I'll see."

The doctor really wanted Clyde to work with these misguided young people.

Clyde told the congregation that Sunday morning, "I'm

expecting some visitors today. And I'd appreciate it if you'd make them feel welcome. I'm going to warn you all that they're not like the folks around here."

The congregation looked at each other, and then turned back to Clyde. He continued, "These kids are long-haired hippies." He waited for that to sort of sink in. Then he went on, "Now, I want you to try to accept them. If they come in bare feet and want to sit on the floor, make them feel welcome. God is bringing them to us, so let's show them that we accept them just as they are."

"But pastor," a young woman spoke up, "I heard that when the sheriff tried to talk with them, they just blew smoke in his face!"

Clyde nodded, "I know. I heard that, too. But if they're coming to hear the Word of God, I don't care if they blow smoke in my face."

Sure enough, the hippies showed up for church. And the congregation embraced them, and treated them with the same warm welcome they gave everyone. These young people definitely were not like our usual worshipers. They wore the whole hippie costume of bell-bottom jeans and tie-dyed shirts, with long hair, headbands wrapped around the top of their heads, and lots of beads. Some of them did in fact show up barefooted. It was clear that they hadn't bathed in awhile, but no one commented on the, shall we say, "interesting" odors that floated off them. The congregation was wonderful on welcoming the hippies to our church.

And as always, God had a plan. Clyde and I told these young hippie people to drop by any time. And they did— every day! Within two months, five of the hippies accepted the Lord Jesus, two brothers, their sister, and two of their friends. Clyde and I worked with them day and night, explaining the love that God had for them, and how fulfilled their lives would be with Jesus in their hearts. I loved every minute of it, and every time we met I saw them respond.

These young hippies just couldn't get enough of the gospel. Eventually three of them went on to the same Bible college Clyde had attended, and from there served the Lord as missionaries in Iran. Another graduated from a different Bible college and went on to a career as a music instructor at a well-known Bible college. The congregation was so proud of their efforts to include the hippies and our children could see what a changed life Christianity had for them.

But this wasn't the only social outcast that Clyde and I worked with in Quincy. The leaders in the community knew that Clyde would work with some of the "hoods" in our town. These were the young boys with criminal pasts, usually not employed, and not particularly motivated but usually spoiling for trouble.

I was always planning creative events at the church. I decided to hold a contest to increase our Sunday morning church attendance, and I wanted to make it really fun. So I copied the Indianapolis 500 as our theme. About this time, Clyde was asked to reach out to one of the leading trouble-makers in own town.

Clyde was driving down the street one day when he saw the young man leaning under the hood of a car. There were several of this young man's buddies all gathered around him. Clyde pulled over, got out of the car, and sauntered up to the group. It was clear who was their leader, but Clyde asked them, "Who's the leader, here."

A thin young man pushed himself back from under the

hood, held out a greasy hand toward Clyde and said, "I am. Want to make something of it?"

Clyde, from his six-foot-two height, looked down at the short, slightly built young man and assessed him to be in his early twenties. He had slicked back dark hair and looked like he could have used a good meal. Clyde answered, "No, I just wanted to know who was in charge, that's all."

The leader put his hands in his pockets, straightened his shoulders, and bouncing from one foot to the other said proudly, "That would be me. I'm Ike." The rest of the group surrounded Clyde in warning, waiting to see what was going to happen. It was clear that Ike had strong leadership qualities with these boys.

Clyde told Ike, "I'm the minister down at the church and we're having a contest this Sunday. We need to break our record." The boys all looked at Clyde with a bored stare. Clyde continued addressing Ike, "Since you're the leader in this part of the community, I thought maybe you could help us out."

Ike pulled a cigarette out of his shirt pocket and lit it. He took a long, slow drag from it, keeping Clyde waiting for a response. Ike blew out the smoke, looked around at his gang of friends, and said, "Sure, I can help. We'll all come." He looked around at the group again and said to them, "Hear that guys? We'll all be there."

And they were! Just on Clyde's single invitation, Ike and several of his friends showed up for church and were well behaved. Our congregation again embraced a group of young people and tried to accept them as they were.

The *Coldwater Daily Reporter* filed a story the following week:

The Rev. Clyde A. Mills smiled happily over having had the largest crowd ever to sit in the pews of the church during its 104 years of existence Sunday.

The theme "Indy 500 Day" was taken from the big race in Indy, but this race was different. This race was to bring people to worship at the church on May 19, with the goal set for five hundred people. The goal was reached and passed.

The bulletin reflected the theme and was written to resemble a race program. The pace car was the choir that led the attending body. The driver of the pace car was the choir director. The starting positions were the hymns sung by the congregation. There were pit stops available and the nursery had powder puff drivers in charge as attendants. An infield pass entitled people to stop outside for coffee following the service.[1]

The next week, Clyde got a phone call telling him that Ike was in jail. Ike was allowed to make only one phone call and he had used it to call Clyde. Clyde drove up to the police station to find out if he could help, to learn that Ike had violated his parole.

Clyde went in to see Ike and seized the opportunity to explain to him that the only way he could lead a straight life was by having God in his life to direct it. Ike was apprehensive, but willing to listen to what Clyde said. He had many questions, but Clyde patiently answered every one of them, returning to visit Ike in jail several times. And then one day, Ike asked Jesus into his life and became a Christian. Ike felt the power of God for the first time.

Clyde learned that Ike could be released from jail if someone would take responsibility for him. Clyde came home to explain to me that he had assumed responsibility for Ike—and I was not happy!

I knew Ike's reputation. But it didn't matter how I felt at that point, because God had His plan in action and I was about to see yet another miracle in our lives.

When Clyde assumed responsibility for Ike it came with some stipulations. Clyde told Ike that he had to get a job, which was not an easy thing to do with Ike's criminal past. But Ike found one; the only problem was that it was twenty-five miles away.

Since part of Ike's parole included that he wasn't allowed to drive, every morning Clyde would drive to Ike's house, make sure that he got up with plenty of time to get ready, and then Clyde drove Ike the twenty-five miles to work. Clyde would drive back home to his office to work his usual workday. Then at about 4:30 p.m., Clyde would drive the twenty-five miles back, pick Ike up, and take him home. During those drives, Clyde and Ike talked about how God was working in their lives. Clyde acted as a personal taxi service for weeks and weeks for Ike, until his parole was up and Ike could drive himself.

I grew to love Ike and enjoyed having him around our home. He had such a fun personality. Ministering to Ike was good for our children so that they could see us work with all kinds of people and that we could enjoy everybody we worked with. Class distinction was not of importance to Clyde or to me, and our children were seeing the value of that.

I remember one of those times when Ike was over, I asked him to stay to eat with us. He agreed to stay, but he was exceptionally nervous. He was fidgety and restless, and couldn't seem to sit still for a minute.

"Goodness, Ike!" I said as I put the salad on the table.

"What's wrong? We're just going to eat a simple meal together with you." Ike sat down at the table and looked up at me, "Mrs. Mills, I've never eaten a meal at a table with a family. I don't know what to do."

I put the salad back in the refrigerator, turned off all the burners on the stove, and put the oven on warm. Dinner could wait. I sat down at the chair next to him, and grasped his hand as Ike went on to tell me of his history. He told me that he had eaten all of his meals in a restaurant from the time he was eleven until now.

Ike had a bitter, sad past that made me wonder about his parents. It seemed that one day Ike came home from school and everybody was gone. "Mrs. Mills, I didn't know what to think. All the furniture was gone. There was just a cot for a bed left behind. They left me!" Ike's family had abandoned him at eleven-years-old.

Ike went on to explain that when that happened it was the middle of a cold Michigan winter. He was all right for a few days, with the little bit of food left in the refrigerator, but then the furnace went out and Ike became very ill.

Thankfully, a neighbor wondered why she hadn't seen any action in Ike's family's apartment. She came in and found Ike extremely ill. Not only was Ike abandoned, cold, and malnourished, he was also sick with infected teeth. The neighbor nursed Ike back to health, but before she could place him in social services, Ike took off to be on his own. I began to realize why Ike was so tough, and my heart ached in sadness for all the love this wonderful young man had to give to a family that didn't want him. He was tough, but he also was very loveable.

Ike eventually married and became a successful businessman who employed several others.

Chapter 20

THE BIRTH OF THE
PASTOR'S WIFE
MINISTRY

O UR CHURCH IN Quincy had a limited budget, but that didn't mean we couldn't have extravagant events. I remember holding a daily vacation Bible School, and making it all up on my own. I held a big fair for the children, with different carnival game booths. I remember the "Guess Your Weight" booth sort of backfired when a woman entered and Clyde guessed about fifty pounds too much. She was so upset, but she still allowed her children to name their new cow "Clyde."

It was there in Quincy that I began to realize I was a good event planner. I discovered that our church was going to be one hundred-years-old. It turned out to be a historical blunder on the part of the church. After I found out that we had missed the centennial of the church by four years, we made up for if with a celebration. I thought, "We have to make this an exciting week of centennial celebration!" I asked all the men to grow beards. I coordinated the seamstresses in the church to make period costumes, and the local newspaper wrote a great article about our church's celebration. There were special events planned for every single day of the week-long celebration.

We held greased pig runs, wheelbarrow races, gunny sack races, and everything was from one hundred years ago. Clyde had a top hat and tails, which he wore to preach on Sunday. Of course, I preferred a more high fashion period style, and I looked like Miss Kitty from *Gunsmoke*. It was a grand celebration and people came from all over to be part of it.

Our church had become a light in the community and it kept growing. The centennial celebration brought more and more people to the church. We outgrew our church building and had to build a new one. One of the couples in the church, George and Nancy Strang, offered the nicest property to build the church. They donated all the land for one dollar to make it legal. It was built by volunteers because so many people were skilled in construction trades. There was great excitement and everybody was involved in it. We would prepare the meals at the church, eat, laugh, and watch God provide for our new building.

Within the year, we moved into a new church home. As we made the move from the old church to the new church we held a formal car caravan. I'll never forget what the oldest member of the church said that day, "Lord, all these people have come in and moved us right out of our church. We love what you're doing, God, so as difficult as it is to say good-bye to the only church I've ever known, we look forward to the future." He was approaching ninety-years-old at the time.

Chapter 21

MINISTERING WITH A FAMILY IN QUINCY: PART I

W E LIVED IN Quincy for twenty-one years. All four of our children grew up there. The little community of Quincy offered our children an opportunity to stand out in many more areas of their lives than if they had grown up in the big city and attended larger metropolitan schools. Like all pastor's children, there were challenges for them, but Clyde and I hoped to teach our children to live up to a standard because they were Christians, not because they were the pastor's children.

I recall a time when the children were playing in the church after a service. They were giggling and racing around the pews when one of those self-appointed "pastor's standards" committee members scolded them. "You can't run in the church, you're the minister's children!" she chided. Clyde was in his office and heard that. He came out and firmly told her, "No, they shouldn't run in the church, but not because they're the minister's children. They shouldn't run in the church because they're Christians, and they should show respect for the church."

Despite the expectation that our children should be role models for the community, I made up my mind that I wasn't going to complain. I knew that Clyde had enough challenges in pastoring that he needed my support, not my complaining. I vowed that I would do the same thing here as I did when Clyde was in Bible college—I would pray, persevere, and not complain.

But I didn't make it. Although Clyde and I would talk about the conflicts, bickering, and discord within the church, we made it a point not to let the children know the difficult situations we faced. We tried to show them only the positive things that would enhance their spiritual maturity.

There was always laughter in our house, especially at the dinner table. Our children embraced the Christian teachings in our home without question. Each of them asked Jesus into their hearts at a young age.

Our oldest son Mike was called into the ministry at age twelve. He knew it was a definite calling. Both his Uncle Wes and Clyde were such strong influences in Mike's life, he recognized God's call before he was a teenager. All of our children realized the excitement of bringing someone to Jesus, and understood how happy Clyde and I were each time we lead someone to the Lord. They wanted to join our mission in life to help others find the joy in being Christians.

The nicest thing about raising our family in Quincy was that it enabled our children to excel in sports. It would have been very difficult in a large area like Grand Rapids, but in Quincy there were small numbers. Mike and Tim excelled in basketball, and Andy earned a football scholarship. Lori was a cheerleader, a volleyball player, a track star, and homecoming queen.

Tim, our youngest, started kindergarten in Quincy. The principal called Clyde one day and asked him to come in for an important conference. We couldn't imagine why.

The principal explained that Tim would get up in front of his class each day and tell how Clyde beat him, sent him to bed without dinner, and was brutal to the other children and to me. When the teacher questioned Tim about it, Tim insisted that it was all true. The principal knew Clyde and doubted Tim's story.

That night, when Tim came home, Clyde put Tim on his knee. Clyde told Tim what the principal had reported and asked, "Tim, did you tell this?"

Tim nodded, "Yes, I did."

Clyde asked, "Did you tell your class that you went to bed without supper?"

Again, Tim nodded, "Yes, Daddy, I did."

Clyde queried a bit more. "Did you tell your teacher that I beat you and your brothers and sister? Did you tell her that I hit your mother?"

Tim squirmed on Clyde's lap. "Yep. I did," he admitted.

Clyde was flabbergasted. "Why?" Clyde asked.

Tim explained casually, "Well, Dad, all the other kids had things to tell at Show-and-Tell, but I didn't have anything, so I just made something up."

We probably should have punished him for the lies, but we laughed and instructed him not to do it again. Tim always had that mischievous charm that was either getting him into or out of trouble. The teachers either loved Tim or hated him for his outgoing personality. One teacher said, "Tim likes to show off." She was right, but so does his mother!

Eventually I grew to love Quincy, and many of the people who started out as my adversaries turned out to be good friends. It was a perfect place to raise our children and I enjoyed watching as all four children grew up there. Three of our children were married right there in Quincy.

The congregation built us a spacious new home about two years after the new church went up. George and Nancy Strang again donated property to build our new house on the most beautiful setting in the entire county, just ninety steps from the church. We had a creek that ran behind our house and a private lake with pine trees, as well. Two of our boys proposed marriage on that lake. We had three of our four children's weddings and wedding receptions there.

As the church grew and the parishioners came to love us, they designed a wonderful surprise for us each fall. It was called "pounding." This was when the church would ask everyone to bring a pound of something for us—a pound of butter, a pound of tomatoes, a pound of salt.

It was an old-fashioned way to stock our cupboards for the winter. But in Quincy it expanded to include things like new tires, sheets, meat, and even cash. It was like Christmas in October. The kids would marvel at the creative ways our wonderful friends would package the gifts. I remember the children digging through the popcorn for hidden money and they learned to inspect any container carefully because usually it held money. How different this was from the liver and tough stewing hens we were first offered!

Chapter 22

MINISTERING WITH
A FAMILY IN QUINCY:
PART II

ONE OF OUR family's most endearing friends in Quincy was Hawley Penn. Hawley was a big developer in the Coldwater area, and looked just like George Burns. He was a self-made entrepreneur and extremely successful.

Hawley's empire crashed with an economic recession and the demise of his marriage. Hawley was devastated with his loss, and Clyde and I took him in. Being in and out of our house over the next few years the children came to think of him as a favorite adopted uncle. He loved to accompany Clyde on hospital calls and they went out for coffee each day. I'd often see Clyde and Hawley returning from Clyde's ministry duties, with Hawley riding shotgun in Clyde's car and Hawley's elbow sticking out the window and a cigar hanging from his lip.

As Hawley recovered both financially and personally, the church became Hawley's new family. Working through his tragedy, Hawley always had the most appreciative spirit toward their love and support.

Hawley demonstrated great lessons to our children. He was the first to admit that he wasn't the perfect Christian, but there was no doubt that Hawley loved the Lord. He told our children, "I ate caviar and I was miserable. Now I eat tuna fish out of the can and I'm happier than I've ever been."

Hawley would set goals for himself. One of his big goals was to stop swearing. Clyde would catch Hawley using salty language and admonish him for it. Hawley was always so sorry and finally vowed that he would not swear on the church property ever again.

~

One day Nancy, our congregation's famous pie maker, brought a fresh strawberry pie to church just for Hawley. She gave it to him just as church was going to start. So Hawley set it on the backseat of his car and went on into the worship service. When church was over, Hawley came outside with all of us to find our Great Dane inside his car. Hawley shouted, and we all turned around in surprise as the big dog looked up innocently from the back seat. All we could see was a big red muzzle with strawberry slobber running down his chest.

Poor Hawley was more upset that he failed in his goal to never swear on church property than he was that he'd lost the pie to our dog. He apologized to Clyde and me for a week afterward.

Hawley had an interesting strategy to help bring people to church. On our Indy 500 attendance event, Hawley and his construction friend Mr. Z held a competition to see who could bring more people to church. Hawley and Mr. Z told their construction crews that they would get their paychecks early if the came to church. Sure enough, eighty-five burly construction workers showed up to help us break our attendance record. Hawley and Mr. Z handed out paychecks after the service.

~

We made it a point with the children that our home would be open for anybody and everybody no matter what the hour was. Clyde and I loved action and wanted our children to enjoy action and be involved. We played a lot of card games and Clyde, being the athlete, trained the children to find sports with their talents. I was never athletic, but I joined in the fun of being the perfect spectator at every event.

Every year we loaded up all the church youth and took them to Gatlinburg, Tennessee, for a retreat. For about a week we'd hike up into the mountains, walk on the rocks where the water falls were, and use that time to help the young people tune out the unimportant and zero in on what was. Clyde and I tried to help them to be strong and not succumb to peer pressure. We always encouraged each of them to go in for a Bible education at least for one year.

Clyde organized young men in the congregation who were interested in the ministry, and offered them the opportunity to hold services in the camp grounds of Marble Lake. These young minister hopefuls brought church to families camped at Marble Lake. They brought music, and the young men had the experience of taking turns preaching at a campground. This opportunity continues today.

Some of our friends from Grand Rapids were excited about what was happening in our little country church. They were pleased and surprised that we were now growing in numbers and in spirituality. These friends would drive back and forth from Grand Rapids for services and to serve. A well-known photographer, Harley Ten Elshof and his wife

Marilyn, would make sure that we had up-to-date pictures every couple years.

Our friends Bill and Bernice would also come to visit often from Grand Rapids. Their daughters were a couple years older than Lori, and always brought her the most beautiful clothes that their daughters had outgrown. These were all from expensive stores and Lori was thrilled that as a result of Bill and Bernice's generosity, she never hurt for fashion. It meant so much to me that Lori could have the latest fashions. And I was thrilled when occasionally Bernice would even bring something for me.

Chapter 23

DADDY

Y FATHER HAD been fighting depression after
retirement. He became immune to the antide-
pressants he had been prescribed. He didn't sleep
well, despite the doctor's care. One day I received a call that
was the most difficult call of my entire life, "You father has
tragically passed away."

I don't even remember who called me, just the sadness
that gripped my heart with the message. When I arrived at
the house I was stunned to learn that Daddy had died by his
own hand.

It was my darkest hour. My sweet, kind, loving father was
gone, and I didn't get to say good-bye.

The next twenty-four hours were, and to this day still are,
a complete blur. Jewish people hold the religious belief not to
practice embalming. So my father was interned the next day.
My father—my Daddy—was the most important man in my
life, next to Clyde. It hurt so much to know that he had been
that depressed. If we were just able to have known how to
help him, or how intense his depression had become, perhaps
things would have been different.

At the funeral, my mother asked Clyde to help officiate.
The rabbi wasn't in favor of this idea, but she insisted. Clyde

gave the eulogy. He prayed about what to say because of the delicate situation of how Daddy had passed away.

Clyde asked my aunts, my sister, and the children and me what their thoughts were when hearing the name, Dave Hyman. All talked about his gentleness, his sweetness, his giving heart. Clyde got up in front of the service and said, "I would like to speak about what I think of when I hear the name Dave Hyman." Then Clyde talked about how he had broken Daddy's heart when he took his young daughter and married her, but how Daddy, as heartbroken as he was, remained kind to Clyde.

Clyde talked about the kind of father Daddy had been to me, and the loving, sweet grandfather he had been to the children. Clyde spoke of how Daddy had left our children with such a rich heritage.

There was much sobbing and crying when Clyde talked about how sorry he was that he had broken Daddy's heart. People were crying and nodding, remembering the drama of our love story.

After the service a man who was the chairman of the synagogue came up to Clyde and hugged him. In his embrace he said, "Clyde, I never knew what a fine man you are; a true man of the cloth. A man of God. I'm so sorry it took twenty-four years for me to realize this." These comments brought soothing comfort to my heart to know that others finally realized what a wonderful, godly man Clyde was.

I stayed with Mother for several days after. As she was cleaning out Daddy's things she said, "I'm going to give you this, and I don't want anybody to ever know about it. It was a poem, folded up in his wallet, with my picture inside the poem. The poem started out, "I counted dollars, while God counted the crosses..." I didn't need to read any other words. I felt that God had given that poem to me as a comfort and a confirmation that my father had made his peace with God. While my heart was still in pieces, I felt a wave of relief wash over me. I wanted to believe that Daddy had come to know the same Messiah that I also knew.

The only comfort I found in my loss was drenching myself in the scriptures. I felt blurry and dazed for a long time. Today it is still a difficult memory and I cannot talk about it.

Despite the circumstances of Daddy's death I was never angry with Daddy. I was just so sorry that he didn't reach out to us for help. If he'd only told us how he was feeling—Clyde, Bedonna, her husband Bob, and I would have done anything to help him.

I went back home and began my daily routine, but with a broken heart. The Lord was my Counselor, and Clyde was my sweet support. The children talked about it, and were concerned for my mother. Fortunately, Mother was a very independent woman who knew how to pick up the broken pieces of her life and continue forward.

Chapter 24

CLOSING THE
CIRCLE UNBROKEN

O N OUR TENTH anniversary of pastoring at the
church in Quincy the congregation gave us a trip
to Israel. Jill Briscoe and her husband Stuart were
hosting a trip to Israel and Jill and I were friends. Jill and
Stuart were outstanding Bible teachers and it worked out that
Clyde and I were able to join their tour. It was on this trip
that my heart went out to Israel and Israel became my love.

Nothing has grounded me more in my Jewish heritage
than touring Israel. The first time I toured the Holy Land it
was almost like becoming a Christian all over again. Walking
the paths of Jesus, touching my feet to the very stones His
feet touched, generated a total renewal of my faith. There was
such closeness to the Lord there; being in the land that He
loved. I was struck by the realization that I have been allowed
to be one of the Lord's chosen people. But I have been chosen
in two ways—one to be born a Jewish girl, and the other by
my choosing to be a Christian.

Visiting my "homeland" has given me new understanding
of my Jewish roots, and an awareness of how the Jewish
people had no home to go to after World War II. I remember
my tears of joy when Israel was established and became a

nation. But I didn't really understand it until I personally visited His land. I realized that God has prepared a special blessing for each person who steps on that ground. And for someone of Jewish heritage, it is remarkable. After my first visit, I vowed that I would do everything I could, with God's help, to promote Israel and support Israel.

Clyde and I learned so much on that first trip and our faith became invigorated with a personal look at the Holy Land. When we visited the Sea of Galilee, Clyde and I got down on our knees in the sand, with the wind blowing in our faces, and we asked God to please make it possible to come back to this land and bring our four children. It was our deepest desire to bring the children to experience the same depth of love for Israel that Clyde and I had discovered.

We returned to Quincy with such joy and excitement about our Israel experience that when we shared it with our congregation they all wanted to take a trip there, too. So I began making preparations to return.

Mother was adjusting to being a widow fairly well, but she was still up to her Jewish-mother tricks with me. If she wanted me to visit, rather than just ask me to come, Mother would find an excuse, like that she didn't have a ride. It was seventy miles to her house, but she thought nothing of asking me to drive over to take her to a doctor appointment or some other errand.

One day, Mother called and asked me to drive her to a luncheon. When I arrived to pick her up, Mother said, "Your Aunt Clara needs a ride, too." So I made a second stop along the way to pick up Aunt Clara, who still resented me for marrying Clyde more than twenty years earlier.

I picked up Aunt Clara and we were on our way to the luncheon, just the three of us in the car. Mother was in the front seat and Aunt Clara in the back seat, when Aunt Clara leaned forward in her seat and poked me in the shoulder and said, "So, you're going back to Israel?"

I smiled, "Yes we are. We're taking the children this time. I'm so excited!" I looked at her in the rear view mirror. Aunt Clara glared back into the mirror at me, "Nu? So!" she raised her eyebrows in challenge, "Did you ever think to take your mother? She's never been, you know!"

Mother was sitting silently across from me, and I saw her squirm in her seat just a bit. I was stunned. It had never occurred to me to invite Mother on a trip with a group of Christians. She had never mentioned wanting to go to Israel.

It made me nervous to even think about it. I glanced sideways at Mother and asked, "Mother, do you want to go?" She glared straight ahead, and out of the side of her mouth she said tersely, "I've never given it a thought. I'll think about it."

As I sat through the luncheon it occurred to me that our trip was planned for a date that would be exactly one year to the day that my father had passed away. Then I remembered that it was traditional for Jewish people to be at the Wailing Wall on the first anniversary of a loved one's death. That's why the term, "Next year in Jerusalem," is used for happy or sad occasions.

I kept wondering through the luncheon, "Would Mother want to go? And what kind of time would she have if she did?" I was embarrassed that I'd never even thought about inviting her before this and I was grateful for Aunt Clara's intervention. The more I thought about it, the more I wanted

Mother to go with us. I knew it would be a special experience to have her there in Israel with our four children.

Throughout the day, I encouraged her to go with us. Each time she'd frown and say, "I'll think about it." She was very noncommittal. When the luncheon was over, I drove Aunt Clara home and then drove back to Mother's house. I had to get back to my family, so I didn't go in with her, I just sat in the car for a few minutes as she gathered her purse, gloves, and keys. As she opened the car door, I said, "Well, Mother, did you think about it?" I was shocked and delighted when Mother said, "Yes! I've decided to go with you."

On the way home I realized that Mother and Aunt Clara had cooked up this plan long before I ever got to Kalamazoo that day. It was a prearranged conversation between them, but it didn't matter to me. I was thrilled that Mother would be going to Israel with her grandchildren.

That night my Aunt Molly called me, excited that Mother was planning this trip with us. "Gerrie, dear, is there going to be room for me to go, too?" The trip was really filled, but I told her that I'd do everything I could to include her. Within a day or two we had cancellations from two people, which were immediately filled by Mother and Aunt Molly. It was all part of God's divine plan.

The day we were getting ready to leave, Clyde took Mother and Aunt Molly aside. Gently he explained to them, "You're both going to hear the name of Jesus on this trip many, many times. It will be mentioned more than you've ever heard before. That name is very sacred to us."

Mother and Aunt Molly didn't say anything; they just looked up at Clyde solemnly. Clyde continued, "We'll take you to everything from the Old Testament; the gardens, the hospital, the Wailing Wall, and of course the Holocaust museum." Mother and Aunt Molly nodded in agreement. I was touched that Clyde was being so kind and sensitive toward their feelings.

Mother's main reason for coming to Israel was to say Kaddish for my father at the Wailing Wall in Jerusalem. To do so would require finding someone who spoke Yiddish. But Yiddish is not a common language in Israel.

Clyde had been scouring the Israeli countryside looking for someone who spoke Yiddish. But every place we went, everyone spoke Hebrew. Mother was getting so discouraged. She could not explain what she wanted in Hebrew, only in Yiddish. But there were no Yiddish speakers to be found. All the people on our tour were feeling bad for her. Clyde and I prayed every day that God would provide someone to assist Mother with her mission.

Mother was excited about going to Jerusalem, but she was also very guarded. When she looked at the itinerary that included the garden tomb after the Wailing Wall, she told Clyde, "When you go to the garden tomb, I'm not going and neither is Molly." Clyde understood and agreed to call a taxi for them at that point of the tour.

It was at the conclusion of the trip when we went up to Jerusalem to pray at the Wailing Wall. We still hadn't located anyone who spoke Yiddish to lead Mother's prayers, but at the entrance to the Wailing Wall, the guide said, "Gerrie, you and your mother go by yourselves. I'll hold the rest of the tour back for a while. You two deserve some time up there alone with each other."

So Mother and I walked along the stone walkway, toward the most holy of holy places for Jews. It was here that Mother and I prayed together for the first time in our lives.

We placed our tiny notes into the crevices of the wall. I held Mother's hand, and with the other hand on the wall I asked, "Who wants to go first?"

Mother softly said, "I will." And she began to pray. Imagine my surprise when Mother prayed that my children would follow in their father's footsteps! It melted my heart. The tears filled my eyes as I listened to Mother's soft voice pray out loud. I know I prayed next, but I was so overcome with joy that I don't even remember what I prayed that day.

After a few moments of silence, Mother and I turned around to head back. We noticed an old woman sitting on the fence that separates the men and women. She had a Babushka tied underneath her chin. Her dark brown skin was creased with deep lines and her hands were gnarled.

My mother took one look at the woman and said breathlessly, "Gerrie. She speaks Yiddish. I can tell." Mother quickly walked over to the woman and started speaking in Yiddish. The woman brightened and raised her hands in excitement, spoke Yiddish back to her, and then she and Mother embraced.

By this time Aunt Molly, Clyde, our children, and the entire tour had walked to the Wailing Wall and were witnessing this meeting. They had all been hoping and praying for Mother to find a Yiddish speaker to help her at this very sight and were sobbing they were so happy for her. We had all watched God's perfect timing, right down to the wire. Mother would have her Kaddish memorial after all. It was such a memorable moment.

In Yiddish the woman said, "Today we break tradition." She called the men across the fence and explained that my father had passed away a year ago, and Mother had traveled from the United States to hold prayers for him.

They nodded and told Mother they would say Kaddish for my father. One man picked up an olive branch, then gathered ten other men around him. Together they prayed as they walked around in a circle. When the men completed their prayers, they walked toward the fence and the leader of the group handed the olive branch to Mother.

Mother was deeply touched. Her tears turned into smiles as she watched the Kaddish ritual. Everyone on the tour appreciated how important this was for Mother and they were honored to have been included.

When it was time for the tour to leave the Wailing Wall, we were going on to visit the garden where Jesus rose from the tomb. Clyde remembered his promise to Mother and Aunt Molly and said, "Mother, I'm going to call a taxi for you and Aunt Molly now. We're going to the garden now." Mother's heart was still touched from her experience at the Wailing Wall and said, "Oh that's all right. I'll go with you."

I said, "Mother, we don't want you to feel that you have to go with us. We'll call a taxi." But both Mother and Aunt Molly insisted that they would be fine to continue the tour. I was really nervous about having them come along. All four of our children would be singing and speaking at this next stop. This would be the most important stop along the entire trip for Christians.

When we got to the tomb, Aunt Molly stood in line to go in to visit the empty tomb. Mother emphatically put her foot down and said, "Molly, you're not going in there!" Challenging Mother's authority Aunt Molly said bravely,

"Sadie, I want to see what's in there," and Aunt Molly got in line and went on in.

Mother was so mad at her! She folded her arms and gave Aunt Molly "the look." I'll never forget when Aunt Molly walked out of the tomb. She was eager to share with Mother.

Molly yelled in a big voice to where my mother was standing off to the side, "Sadie, I looked in, there's nothing there!" Truer words were never spoken—that tomb is empty because our Lord is risen.

I don't think Mother objected to the children singing and speaking that day. But if they hadn't been her grandchildren she would have. Aunt Molly loved it, but if either of them experienced any emotional impact from these moments they kept it to themselves. But my life and the lives of my children were touched that day.

When we returned, Clyde and I immediately began making plans for the next trip. To date, Clyde and I have visited Israel seven times and are presently coordinating an eighth trip.

Chapter 25

MASSACHUSETTS MASSACRE

CLYDE AND I attended the National Prayer Breakfast in Washington DC and there we met a group of people from New England who were looking for a pastor to start a church. They said, "We'd like to move our mountains for God. We'd be interested in having you as our pastor."

Clyde and I had been in Quincy for twenty-one years. At first we wouldn't even consider leaving. But they pursued us, and we prayed and felt as if God was leading us. The church leaders told us, "We need you to help us move the mountains for God in Massachusetts."

Saying good-bye to Quincy was the hardest thing we'd ever done. We had been there for twenty-one years; our children had grown up there. The people in Quincy loved us as much as we loved them, but Clyde and I wanted to be open to whatever God had for us.

Despite being convinced that Clyde was lead by the Lord, things were strained from the start. After Clyde and Tim's first Elders board meeting at the new church, Clyde got into the car, gripped the steering wheel, and looked at Tim, "Pull up your bootstraps, son. We're in for a tough ride here." Little did we know how rough that ride would be.

The church grew to ninety members in no time, but Clyde and the existing church leadership team were not compatible. It's a part of my life that was very painful. It wasn't all bad times there; seeing the church grow and seeing people accept the Lord is always gratifying.

Tim and Clyde could both tell that these men of leadership had a different countenance here than they did when they came to Quincy to recruit them. These men had a preconceived idea of what they wanted their church to be. They didn't want the pastors to lead policy, or to even use their interpretation of the board's instruction.

Clyde and Tim just continued doing the best that they could. The church took off and began growing quickly. Clyde and Tim invited everyone, from all walks of life to worship with us. But the Board didn't want just anybody to come to their church. They wanted people to come who were professionals. They sought prominent people with social status.

We were located in New England, where so many of these dear people were not even familiar with the gospel message. We knew that God had sent us there to deliver His message, so we proceeded to spread the good news accordingly. After a few months, one of the men who was backing the church financially called Clyde and said, "I've found the house for you!"

When he gave Clyde the address, Clyde recognized the upscale neighborhood and asked, "Isn't that on the hill?" The board member said, "Yes! Just come and see it!"

This was during the same time the Jim and Tammy Baker scandal of extravagance had broken in the news. Reluctantly,

Clyde went to meet with him. I followed with Mike and Ellen who were visiting. I can remember this mansion vividly. It had a huge central hallway with several large living and family areas, two offices, a library, an extravagant kitchen, pantry, and laundry areas. There was a sweeping staircase that led to five bedrooms, five baths, and five fireplaces. There were even servant's quarters. This was supposed to be a house for just Clyde and me!

As I walked in I heard Clyde say, "This house is way too big and too pretentious for people to walk into and feel comfortable."

"But this is the kind of house you need to live in to appeal to people that we're recruiting to our church," the board member insisted.

"I want people to be able to come into my home, kick of their shoes, sit down on the sofa, have a Coke and watch the ball game," explained Clyde.

I started looking around. "How would I clean this place?" I asked.

The board member was irritated. "Hire a servant to live in. Make it a bed and breakfast as well." That was the last thing I wanted to do! My idea of making breakfast is a protein drink or a bowl of cereal.

I looked up at Mike and Ellen leaning over where they wouldn't be seen. They were both shaking their heads, no, no, no.

This man was unfamiliar with not getting his own way. He told us to think about it. He called Clyde that evening, "Clyde, what did you think about buying the house?" he demanded.

"I don't think a lot of people would feel comfortable coming to see us in that house," Clyde explained.

The board member rallied, "That's the kind of people we want at our church. We want the bankers, the lawyers, you know, the professional people."

Clyde retorted, "Well, I want the candlestick makers. And whoever God leads me to bring."

The house continued to be a pressing issue for the board. But when they wanted Clyde and me to assume a mortgage for this monster and the church would make the payments as our housing allowance we knew this was not of God. The utility bills alone would be more than what a normal rent would be!

Things got worse. The board instructed Clyde not to hand out any literature that used terms like *born again* or *saved*, and didn't want him to speak those terms in his sermons, either. More and more the board was trying to dictate how Clyde could minister to the people.

Finally, at a meeting, Clyde explained that his ministry was directed by God, not by man. He explained that using phrases like *born again* or *saved* was what he had been called to do. The board would not honor Clyde's conviction and finally Clyde simply resigned for himself and for Tim, effective immediately.

The board was incredulous! They didn't expect Clyde to just quit and they did everything they could to encourage Clyde to stay. They kept calling, coming over, regretting the way they had tried to influence him. Finally, they gave Clyde and Tim each a generous financial severance package.

I respected Clyde's decision and supported his position, but this was unnerving. I prayed in earnest for God to direct us, but I also drowned my stress in chocolate pudding. From the moment that Clyde told me he'd resigned, until we were on the road to leave, I went into the kitchen, took out my chocolate pudding mix, and made pudding a couple times a day. I cooked it and ate the whole batch hot, time after time.

We called Mr. Miles, the president of Clyde's Bible college in counsel. When Clyde told him we'd resigned, Mr. Miles interceded immediately, "I have an apartment right here at the school. I want you and Gerrie to feel free to use this as long as you need it."

With no place to go it was as good of a destination as we could get. But we needed to be moved out of the church's house immediately. How could we move our household in two days?

Our son Mike was in Michigan. He called Rick, the husband of a girl who grew up in our church, who owned a large trucking company. Mike asked Rick if he ever went to Massachusetts.

Rick responded, "Nope, never have. I only go south and to the Midwest."

Mike thanked him and tried to think of another avenue to help us. About an hour later Mike's phone rang. It was Rick.

"How fast can your folks be ready?" Rick asked. "I'm going to send a truck to Boston, for the first time ever. I'm going to drop off my load of produce and then drive to their house with an empty truck."

Mike said, "Send it!" And Mike and a friend jumped into the car and drove all the way out from Michigan to Massachusetts to help us load up. When they arrived I was still making pudding.

I was in a daze. Clyde had never been without work a day in his life. This whole situation was even more complicated because Clyde had included Tim's resignation, without consulting him while he was away at a wedding in Michigan.

Clyde went over to Tim's' house and packed everything he and Michelle owned into barrels. Dishes and bras went into the same barrel.

Many of the wives of the board members were sick about what happened, and helped me pack. But the one that helped the most was the very man and woman that they didn't want to come to our church. It was the man who ran the riverboat, who had a tooth missing in front, and didn't dress appropriately according to their standards. He and his wife helped us pack, load, and do whatever we needed done. God will reward them with a special star in their crowns.

We moved to Michigan into Mr. Miles apartment in record time. Clyde went to work immediately to help Mike with his ministry. He took over a lot of the administration, helping Ellen, as Mike went out speaking.

Mother's lessons in frugality paid off. We lived on our savings. The sad truth was that Clyde was no longer interested in being a pastor. Eventually we moved into a townhouse, where Clyde set up an office in the basement and studied every day that he wasn't helping Mike.

One day Mr. Miles was over, and I showed him Clyde's office. Mr. Miles grinned at me, "It won't be long, Gerrie. He'll be pastoring again. It's his calling."

That encouraged me. I just kept praying, "Lord, what do You want us to do?" The only comfort in this disconsolation was that we were back in Grand Rapids, surrounded by wonderful Christian friends who were understanding and supported our call.

Bill and Bernice, our Arab friends, wanted to encourage us. We socialized with them often. Bernice treated me to lunch regularly. She held me up in prayer and in friendship, calling me daily, listening to my concerns and assuring me that God would answer one day soon.

Clyde was still uncertain where God would lead him. I felt in limbo. The events back east had really shaken me. My faith wasn't shaken, and I knew that God had allowed it to happen for a reason, but I didn't know the reason. Our friends did everything they could to encourage us. I felt useless and unsettled in my ministry, even though I was serving. I look back on it now and refer to this time as my "Desert Experience."

Clyde had resigned in November and the following Mother's Day we had a special service where babies were dedicated to the Lord. On the way home, Clyde said to me, "I feel somewhat lead to begin exploring to see if God would have me go back into pastoring."

I was thrilled beyond words! I knew what a wonderful pastor Clyde was. And apparently his bruises were healing. Clyde still needed to have his confidence back, but God was healing his heart.

I had been practicing a ministry along side Clyde since the day we were called together. I was ready to get back out there and serve as a pastor's wife, and I wanted Clyde's calling to be validated by God again soon. I wanted to belong, I wanted to be needed, I missed being a leader, and I laid it all down at the feet of the Lord.

Chapter 26

HEAVEN ON EARTH—
IN NAPLES, FLORIDA

B Y THIS TIME, all our children were grown and
married. Mike was ministering in Grand Rapids and
Tim and Michelle lived there, too. Andy and Cathy
were in the Midwest; Lori and Mark were living in Canada.
Mother was still living in Kalamazoo. With the adjustment
from leaving Massachusetts, I'd come to deeply appreciate
the support and love of having family around us.

Mike had a friend who knew someone looking for a
pastor in Florida. They interviewed Clyde on the phone and
then flew us down to meet them. I was delighted that Clyde
was seeking if God would have him pastor again. We were
already in love with Florida, since we'd vacationed there
many times.

While we were there interviewing, we stayed in a real nice
hotel. I remember Clyde floating on his back in the ocean,
grinning mischievously and saying, "Please Lord, please,"
toward the heavens.

Clyde and I loved Florida. It was one of our favorite places
in the United States. Only the Lord could develop the circumstances to open a door to send us to work in a beautiful place

like Naples, Florida. God made it so clear that we just walked right through.

When we arrived, it was easy to see that there was work to be done in Naples. But in my heart, I didn't want to leave my family behind to do it. I was praying, asking for God's guidance, concerned that this meant leaving all of our children behind. This was a sacrifice for me. I'd never been away from all our children before. As much as we loved Florida, it seemed like it was the farthest place we could go from our children and grandchildren.

I mentioned this to Mr. Miles one day and he said to me, "Gerrie, ministry is a sacrifice." It hurt, but I never forgot it.

We accepted the call, and Clyde and I packed up our belongings and headed for the Sunshine State. One of my first days of devotions in Naples, I was sitting outside under our tree, when I came to Nehemiah 6:15, "So on October 2 the wall was finished—just fifty-two days after we had begun." These words floated around inside my head a bit, when I wondered how many days it had taken to get me here in Florida. I took out my calendar, and counted back. I realized it was fifty-two days from the initial interview until Clyde and I felt confirmation that we should answer the call to Florida.

In the call vote at the new church, it was unanimous to call Clyde, with the exception of one no vote. A few months later, there was a knock on Clyde's door, and a woman we'd come to know through church named Sherry asked, "May I come in?

Clyde invited her in and she sat down nervously. "I have a confession to make," she told us. "I was the one no vote."

Clyde and I looked at each other in wonderment. But Sherry explained, "In my defense, I want you to know that

I voted no because I didn't have enough information to vote yes. The day you were visiting, no one showed up to help me in the nursery. I was busy taking care of babies. I was trying to listen in the hallway to the sermon, but I had to rush back inside to take care of the babies. When the church called for a vote, I didn't think I'd heard enough or knew enough about you. I didn't have enough information to vote yes, and I didn't know you could abstain." Tears rolled down Sherry's cheeks.

"It's all right," Clyde told her.

Sherry sniffled, "I felt so guilty at the welcome party. I developed a really bad headache. And then Gerrie brought me some aspirin and I'd voted no on your call! My head was hurting because I was stressed out from being the only no vote."

Clyde and I chuckled as Sherry sniffed to Clyde, "I think so much of you and Gerrie, I wish I had never been the no vote." We laughed together as Sherry felt the burden leave her in forgiveness and Clyde teased her from that day by calling her "Sherry-no-no."

Sherry became the most active member in our church. Her musical talents enhanced our services and she looked for ways to serve in every avenue of ministry she could serve in and to also help us.

Naples was an interesting socioeconomic community. It was made up of "snowbirds" who came to Florida for the winter months and families who lived in Florida year-round.

I found Florida to be paradise. I loved the beach, the clean sand, even the humidity. I loved the beautiful condominium that Clyde and I bought, and the glitzy lifestyle Naples offered. The only thing I needed in Naples was more help in the church. There was so much to do and God had a special plan for that.

Naples was the most beautiful place I'd ever seen and the "honeymoon" period as a pastor lasted for a while. By then some of the people who had left the church under the last pastor decided to come back with the new pastor. After all the challenges we'd faced in the past, Clyde thought he could handle almost anything, but things in Naples proved him wrong.

The "group" of returnees had already been to every other church in Naples, and it didn't take long for Clyde to realize this group was going to seriously challenge us. When we were on vacation, someone called a lady who considered herself "the same qualifications as the pastor" to get our phone number. Instead of giving out a number where Clyde could be reached she said, "Oh, you talk to me. I'm a better counselor and more knowledgeable than Pastor Mills."

This woman had asked Clyde if she could teach a Bible class on Sunday nights. Clyde told her he'd pray about it and get back to her. But when we returned from vacation Clyde discovered she'd already started the Bible class before the Sunday evening service, and had encouraged people in that class to skip the evening service.

Once she called a speaker to tell him what to preach on for his message, acting as if it was Clyde's request. Her bold disregard for the actual leadership in the church was a grave concern for Clyde and the board knew that this woman had to be dealt with. Eventually she was asked to leave our church.

When she left, all the pastors in Naples were fearful that she might return to their churches. She'd caused so many problems that when she moved to another town, every pastor was relieved. When she left, the rest of her "group" followed. Suddenly things looked brighter in our church in Naples. That was when the dearest friends of our lives came to Naples for the winter and chose our church.

~

Florida offered me a whole new wardrobe opportunity. No longer did I need warm woolen coats or turtleneck sweaters. Now I needed summer clothing, twelve months of the year. When I was at the country club one day, I noticed a woman in one of the cutest summer styles I'd ever seen. I told my friend, "Trade places with me, I want to sketch her outfit."

She was wearing black and white polka dots on a lightweight sleeveless top, with an adorable black-and-white polka-dot skirt. The outfit was interesting with two different sizes of dots. She had shoes to match and even polka dot earrings. I set off on a mission to copy her style and I could hardly wait for the next opportunity to wear it.

That Sunday I was so proud of myself, looking so stylish and smart in my polka dots. When I turned around in church, I saw her, sitting a few rows back from me on the other side, dressed in the outfit I had so carefully copied. I tried to pretend that I didn't notice our similar outfits, but when she greeted Clyde after church, he made the faux pas of complimenting her with, "My you look nice today. My wife looks just like you!"

She called me the next day. "I think we have a lot in common," she said cheerfully. "I'd like to take you to lunch. Let's go shopping together." That was the beginning of one of the most endearing friendships of my lifetime. Peggy Hamstra and her husband Wilburt became tennis partners and our constant companions.

When Wil and Peggy found out that our children were spread around the country and hadn't been together in nine years, they offered us the use of their home on Lake Charlevoix, in Michigan.

"It's big enough for you all," Peggy encouraged. "Why don't you use it?"

So Mike, Andy, Lori, and Tim, their spouses, and their children came from all parts of the country to Michigan to meet Clyde and me for a family reunion on Lake Charlevoix.

I'll never forget our daughter-in-law, Cathy, pouting in the back seat of her car, "I'm not going to stay in some flea-bitten place," Cathy warned. "It's so far out here, who knows what kind of dump we'll find?"

Our car caravan started driving down a mile long driveway. Just about that time we broke over the crest of a hill where we could see through the pine trees, there was Peggy and Wil's home, a fabulous dream of a log home, standing stately on the edge of a large lake. The mansion was complete with two full-time caretakers, three beaches, motorboats, spacious decks, and a wraparound front porch with beautiful landscaping. This gift from Peggy and Wilburt was one of my favorite blessings from Naples.

~

I made friends quickly in Naples and soon realized that I was surrounded by some of the most unique, dynamic Christian fellowship of my life. In Naples our relationships were so intimate and we felt like family overnight.

Tish was in her early thirties, a bright, attractive business executive who drove into the church parking lot and saw me walking one day. She wanted to know more about our church. Eventually Tish became involved in our Youth Ministry and she moved into the condo above our home.

Tish was the project manager of Westin Resort, and she made it possible for Clyde to golf any day he wanted to *for free* at the end of his workday. Tish had been divorced, and after her divorce accepted the Lord. One day Tish received a phone call from Gunars, her former husband, telling her that he, too, had become a Christian. Tish was happy for him, but ended the conversation quickly. She didn't want to talk with him one minute further.

But Gunars was persistent and called again and again asking to see her. Tish finally said, "All right," with all the disgust that she could muster.

Gunars showed up and told Tish that he was sorry for how their marriage had ended. Clyde and I met Gunars and we found him to be a nice, responsible young man who was truly sorry for how he had hurt Tish in their marriage. Tish was upset that we liked him so well. It irritated her even more that all the kids in the church youth group adored him, too.

It was New Years Eve when despite herself, it was clear that Tish's feelings began to rekindle with Gunars. Both of them tried several more times to reconcile, but resigned themselves finally that their feelings were over.

Tish was so glad. She took a job in Vale, Colorado, but didn't tell Gunars that she was moving. The night that the movers were at Tish's condo, Gunars called. He said he was sure that he and Tish would get back together because he'd had a dream. He went on to explain the dream to Tish, saying that Jesus was in the dream and had asked Gunars why he was afraid of the Bridegroom.

Tish yelled at Gunars over the phone, "Don't you ever call me again, because I had the same dream last night!" She slammed the phone down on him and told me, "It's over. We're done. We're finished." Somehow I didn't think so. Tish loaded everything into the moving van and left for Vale.

Tish stayed in touch with me when she moved from Vale to Orlando. There she started seeing a counselor to sort out her feelings for Gunars. The counselor agreed with all the reasons Tish didn't want to reunite with Gunars. Tish was so relieved that the counselor agreed with her. But then, the counselor asked Tish if Jesus would have forgiven Gunars for the mistakes in their marriage. Through this counselor and a great deal of prayer, Tish was able to forgive Gunars.

Ten years after their divorce the couple remarried. They are now happily located in Dallas, the proud parents of two beautiful children.

Dolly and her companion Hal drove into the Naples church parking lot in a big, new, blue Lincoln Continental. After the service, she went right up to Clyde and said, "I want to become a Christian." This was music to a pastor's ears. He invited her and Hal into his office, but Hal refused. After a bit of discussion Dolly talked Hal into joining her, and they met with Clyde in the office. Dolly had been very wealthy growing up as a Coca-Cola heiress. She realized that possessions were not satisfying. When she understood that Jesus could give her a profound purpose to her life and also forgive her of her entire past, she eagerly accepted Him into her heart and life.

So excited was Dolly, with her newfound faith, that she and Hal also purchased a condo right above us. Dolly was energetic and enjoyed evenings much more than mornings. I am a morning person and go all day, crashing in exhaustion at night. Dolly preferred to sleep late into the morning and be up most of the night. Having her right above us was a challenge.

I began to get to know Dolly, and learned that she'd been married several times and had had a very difficult life. Now that she was a Christian, she wanted to marry Hal a second time. She confided in me that they'd been married and divorced.

One day, Clyde was talking with them, and Liz Taylor had just gotten another divorce. Dolly asked Clyde, "How many times do you think I've been married?" Clyde cautiously answered, "I don't know Dolly, three or four?" She looked at him and shook her head. "Up," she answered. Clyde was surprised. "Five or six?" he asked. "Up," Dolly gestured with her hands. Clyde frowned. "Seven or eight?" he ventured. Dolly grinned, lifting her palms toward the ceiling, "Up." Clyde tipped his head to the side, "Nine or ten?" Dolly continued to grin. "Up," she replied.

Clyde didn't know where this conversation was going. "Dolly, eleven? Twelve?"

Dolly put her hands down. "Hal will be my thirteenth husband," she said excitedly, "because we've decided we're going to be remarried."

It turned out that Dolly loved weddings and she asked me to help her plan number thirteen. It was a fun day, and I will always remember Dolly with a deep fondness in my heart for she was a loveable eccentric. She had grown up demanding everything her way and because of her extreme wealth, getting it. Becoming a Christian helped Dolly recognize the needs of others and enriched her life.

Hal was transferred to Homestead, Florida, three weeks before hurricane Andrew struck. Dolly's first words, after they lost everything in the storm were, "What would I have done without the Lord? He's helped me through this tragedy." It made me so grateful that Clyde and I had spent so much time with Dolly and Hal as they began their lives as new Christians.

~

When I was out speaking on a traveling tour, I spoke at a ladies retreat in Indiana where I met Cherie Leone. She was the hostess of the event. She and husband Lou had decided to retire early from living in New York City. They were trying to decide where to start a new life after a successful career with Magnavox. Both Lou and Cherie leaned toward Florida to make their new start. When Lou came alone to Florida to survey the area he met with us. Then he called Cherie and told her, "I've found our new home. This is where I want to come and help with this church."

Lou and Cherie sold everything and bought a condo about a mile from us, and jumped into service at the church immediately with both feet. We were inseparable from the day they arrived. A few months later, we received a phone call to learn that Lou had crashed in his airplane and was killed instantly.

To this day we're so grateful that we were able to know him so well. After he passed away, we took Cherie into our home for months. She couldn't be in her home alone, she was missing Lou so much. She and Lou had only been Christians for seven years.

Cherie had been away when Lou's accident happened. When they were bringing her home, she was asked what she expected to find there. I'll never forget her answer, "There will be the Bible open on the breakfast table, and a copy of the devotional *Our Daily Bread*." When Cherie walked in, she found the Bible open and the devotion beside it. The *Daily Bread* article that day was about a pilot preparing for a flight.

Sherry, from our Naples church, tells it this way: "I think their biggest ministry was within our church family. We were always doing something together. Clyde and Gerrie were always bringing new Christians in to the church, but there was such deep fellowship. They made Christianity fun. Most of us had never experienced that. We didn't realize that we could be Christians and have so much fun. The fellowship that we had, we couldn't wait to get together with them again."

The next nine years was living in paradise with the sweetest Christian friends a pastor and wife could ever ask for. They were all mature Christians, supportive of the church mission, with positive outlooks, and they appreciated one another as well as Clyde and me. We laughed a lot together and there was a creative energy that welcomed the new adventures in ministry each day.

While there was a great deal of wealth in our church, most of our members didn't view themselves as wealthy. They saw themselves as people who had been entrusted with funds by God and wanted to share it however God planned. There were so many couples that enriched our lives in Naples, and who also helped us when we moved from Naples: Dave and Joan, Jerry and Sherry, Don and Joyce, Will and Peg, Bob and Edna, and John and Mae, and many more too numerous to name.

Every day in Naples, I'd walk outside and I would lift my hands up into the air and say, "Naples, I never take you for granted."

The best thing about living in Naples was the seven miles of beautiful beaches we had access to. Clyde and I would visit the beach often, holding hands as we'd walk and pray together with the water lapping over my toes. We'd begin at Thirty-second Street, which bordered the beach with luxury mansions, walk three miles to the pier, and then back as part of our routine. By this time in my life I had come to expect answered prayer, but nothing prepared me for the way God answered my prayer on this day.

It was really hot this particular day, and Clyde decided to take a dip. I sat on the beach with my toes in the sand, watching him. He walked far out into the surf, more than a city block, then he turned left and plunged into the surf, swimming, bobbing in and out of the waves like some kind of dolphin.

I took such pleasure in watching Clyde splash around out there like a kid, since he enjoyed the water so much. When Clyde had tired and had enough swimming, he walked back to the beach.

We proceeded to walk on up the shoreline, playing tag with the waves and enjoying our time together. I noticed Clyde fumbling in the pockets of his bright yellow bathing suit. He reached down into one, then into the other, pulling the pockets inside out.

Finally, Clyde looked at me, "Gerrie, I've got something to tell you."

I looked up at him curiously. "What?" I asked.

"I lost my keys out there," Clyde said penitently.

It took a minute for that to register. "Out there" had to mean out in the surf about three blocks back on the shoreline. "You mean out there in the water?"

"I'm afraid so," Clyde said.

"Why would you even have your keys out there?" I questioned.

Clyde shrugged his shoulders. "My pockets were deep; I thought they'd be safe."

I looked around the desolate beach. We were fairly isolated, and there were no familiar faces to be found. "What are we going to do?" I asked Clyde. The key ring held our car keys, house keys, church keys, and every key we used. But the biggest immediate issue was not being able to get into our car to drive home.

Clyde shook his head, "I don't know."

Our car was parked a good two miles away from where we were on the beach. In the nearby neighborhood of multi-million dollar estates it was completely inappropriate to knock on a door for help. We were far way from a public phone and it was long before everyone carried a cell phone. I realized that neither Clyde nor I even had any money between us, and I could just picture someone when I asked to borrow a quarter in this neighborhood!

I took a deep breath of faith. "Clyde, I'll start praying; you go out in the surf and look for those keys."

Clyde looked at me like I was crazy. We weren't even sure where along the shore Clyde had ventured out into the water.

"Please?" I pleaded. "Please!!"

Clyde nodded and we turned around and headed back to where we hoped was the right spot to begin looking for the keys. The tide had the water churned up to a murky blue green, and the sun burned down through the clouds.

Clyde went out into the surf and walked way out to about the same city block distance he had before. As he walked along, I paced on the beach, praying. I could see Clyde, diving down into the water, and trying to press his feet into the sand.

I was tense, pacing back and forth along the beach, with my hand over my eyes, "Lord, if You help him find these keys, I'll tell everyone for the rest of my life how You answer prayer. All the praise will go to You!"

I'd stop, look out at Clyde exploring the bottom of the ocean, pushing doubts away, and return to my pacing. My prayer continued, "Nothing is too difficult for You, Lord. The prayer of a righteous woman availeth much. I need to avail, Lord."

I paced some more, placing my hand over my eyes and petitioned God to help us, "With God all things are possible. Please make this a 'possible.' We do the possible Lord, and You do the impossible. Nothing can be more impossible that this, but I know You can help Clyde find those keys!"

I looked out at Clyde again. I saw him bring something to the surface, then saw him toss it aside, knowing it was a rock or a seashell. The playful water was the same marine jeweled tones, swirling with the tide, but now it had lost its magic and seemed ominous. Clyde continued to walk along the bottom of the ocean, diving down in search of the car keys.

I returned to my pacing, petitioning God to answer my prayer, "Lord, I know You can help us, You have answered so many prayers for me in my lifetime. I ask You to answer this one today." I stopped pacing and looked out at the sea once again.

There was Clyde, chest deep in the water, patiently searching where he hoped was the right spot on the Atlantic floor. He stepped out and moved his foot around in the sand, and stopped. I saw him dive down, and come up with something in his hand.

He turned and waved to me on the beach, holding the keys over his head! Clyde had found the lost keys!

I screamed, "Yes Lord! Yes! Another answered prayer!"

When Clyde got to the shore with the keys, I threw my arms around him, and kissed him.

"Nothing short of a miracle, Gerrie," Clyde said to me, "we've had nothing short of a miracle today."

I looked out at the ocean we loved to visit and felt the presence of God shining down on us through the cracks in the clouds over the frothy, aquamarine water. Clyde was right, we had just experienced a miracle, and I could hardly wait for the next one.

Chapter 27

RETIREMENT—NOT IN NAPLES, FLORIDA

AT SIXTY-FIVE CLYDE decided it was time to retire. Florida was a perfect place to do just that. But a month after retirement, discontent surfaced when Clyde and I were sitting on the beach, watching the waves roll in. We were slathered in sun tan lotion, eating Danish, sipping coffee, and sharing the newspaper and our Bibles. Clyde leaned over and kissed me and said, "Gerrie, I miss being needed." "I've got too much energy and good health to be retired."

After praying about it, we decided to return to Michigan and help Tim and Mike with their ministries. We kept our condo in Florida to return to, and we went up to Michigan where Tim had rented a small apartment for us that came with the office they used. This was our new two-room home. It was like going from paradise to the Arctic—we were back to frigid, icy Michigan weather with an upstairs outside entrance.

But it was all part of God's plan.

While we were in Michigan, Clyde and I flew to California to visit Lori and Mark and the grandchildren. We wanted to see the new church they'd planted in a little town called

Rocklin, near Sacramento. While there, we took a drive to a nearby town, which seemed to me to be hours away. Actually, it was only twenty minutes from Mark and Lori's house.

Mark is a wonderful visionary. As he drove the countryside he pointed to a dry field and said, "Over in those fields there will be a big retirement center, called Sun City Lincoln Hills." All I could see in the fields were dead grass, rocks, coyotes, jackrabbits, and an empty rodeo grounds.

"I'd love to see you start a church out here at this retirement center," Mark said excitedly, with Lori nodding in agreement. Not being the visionary that Mark is, I couldn't imagine that anything would be built out here. And there wasn't anything to start a church with. There were no houses, no people. Nothing.

Then he drove into the town of Lincoln. There were three things that stood out in my mind coming from glitzy Naples: a Burger King restaurant, a small independent grocery store that had dirty windows, and the Gladding McBean factory where they manufactured clay sewer line pipes. To me Lincoln looked like fast food, grimy windows, and dirty red debris.

I thought to myself, "Are you out of your mind, Mark Welch? I would not leave Naples for something like this! In fact, I don't want to leave Naples period!"

I listened to Clyde, Mark, and Lori rattle on about what all could be taking place in this new development. I didn't believe it could possibly happen. Mark predicted that there would be ten thousand people here within the next ten years. We drove back to Lori's house and I thought that was the end of that.

We came out again to California several months later. Mark said, "Mom, remember the new Sun City I showed you that was going up in Lincoln?"

I looked at him and scowled, "Yeah."

Mark grinned. "Well, wait till you see the model homes park!"

So, to humor him I went with him back out to see it. It seemed like it took forever to drive that fifteen miles because it was so desolate out there. But when we got there, I was surprised to discover that Mark was right. The new homes were beautiful! But I was shocked to learn that the home prices in Sun City Lincoln Hills were about twice as expensive as homes were in Naples.

When we decided that we'd be open to moving to California, Clyde and I sought the advice and counsel of Wilburt.

"Well, what do you think about it, at our ages starting a church from scratch, knowing nobody?" Clyde asked him.

Wilburt was a developer and successful businessman. He sat back in his chair and replied, "I think it would be great."

We explained to Wilburt that we'd have to purchase a home in California, where the real estate values were much higher than Florida. Wilburt told us the pros and cons of that. When it came to raising support, Wilburt told us he wanted to be the first to help us.

Once we arrived in California, Wilburt and Peggy supported us for years, along with Don and Joyce, Dave and Joan, and Jerry and Sherry, until the church was well established. It felt good to tell all our friends in Naples that their support wouldn't be necessary anymore. How unusual it was for a pastor to leave (and the congregation didn't want him to leave) but the congregation extended themselves and their resources to support our move away from them as far away as California.

When God seemed to be nudging us to serve in California it was so hard to sign a mortgage agreement at our ages. But we knew that if we were to plant a church in this community, we needed to live here. We told Mark and Lori we would pray about it. Then we met with Dr. Steve Babby, who was the district superintendent for the Wesleyan Denomination for Southwest District.

I went in to this meeting with trepidation, because Clyde and I had never served under a specific denomination in our entire ministry. But Dr. Babby came highly recommended by Mark and Lori, and when Dr. Babby and his wife Barbara met Clyde and me with such warmth and encouragement, I knew this was where God would have us serve. Dr. Babby's leadership has inspired many pastors in his district and Clyde felt confident that he could begin to plant a new church in Lincoln Hills. Imagine, just six years later, Dr. Babby awarded Clyde with the Pastor of the Year honor for the entire district. Clyde and I have met the finest qualities of pastors and pastors' wives under Dr. Babby's leadership and are honored to be included in this ministry.

Dr. Babby told us he'd be glad to have us aboard, and welcomed us. It meant raising support to start a new church, a new concept for Clyde and me. We'd always pastored at existing churches in the past. The challenge looked better to Clyde than it did to me. I didn't want to leave Florida and I didn't want to go into debt for an uncertain future.

We flew back to Michigan, picked up our car, and proceeded to drive back to Florida. On the way home, we ran into the most horrible blizzard and traffic was bumper to bumper. Clyde said, "Gerrie, this will be a good time for us to pray."

I knew what he meant. First I looked at Clyde and then out the window. He took my hand and said, "Gerrie, we need to seek out what the Lord would have us do."

I had never felt so resistant as I did at that moment. And it was all because I didn't want to leave my beautiful home in Naples. I feel so guilty about that now, but it just reveals to me how wrapped up in my wants I can be.

So Clyde prayed, asking God to reveal to us what His perfect will would be for us, as husband and wife, in establishing a new church in Lincoln Hills. While he was praying, I was praying with him, but still envisioning the Gladding McBean factory, Burger King, and small grocery. It was still not my idea of a good place to live.

When Clyde finished praying, he squeezed my hand and said, "Gerrie, you need to pray." Uh-oh—I'd have to be honest. I prayed as honestly as I could, "I don't want to leave Naples, Lord," I prayed tearfully. "I don't want to leave my house. But I'm willing if this is really what You want for us, I mean *really* what You want, I know You can change my heart. You're going to have to help me to be more willing than I am now. You need to make it ever so clear, Lord." I sniffled a bit and continued, "I'd love to be near Lori and in the same state with Andy and Cathy. But Lord, my desire would be to keep our home and just try it out in California, and not make the move permanent to start."

At this point in our lives, our home in Naples was paid for, and it was a perfect set up for a retirement couple. Real estate in California was much more expensive than in Florida.

Moving to California meant a huge financial risk this late in our lives. Despite my faith, and being grounded in confidence that the Lord would provide, I was being selfish in not wanting to let go of the security of having our home paid for in Naples. At the same time, I wanted Clyde to have fulfillment.

We drove all the way to Florida that day. When we arrived, I was so glad to be back in my beautiful, spacious condo. I was tidying everything up, and doing the washing. At 1:30 a.m. Clyde called, "Gerrie, come to bed, it's been a long day."

The next morning when the phone rang, a woman said, "I understand you're contemplating a move to California. Is your home going to be for sale?"

I was at a loss for words. Clyde had heard the conversation and shook his head yes, and I shrugged my shoulders as if to say, "I don't know."

I said, "Well, maybe. We might consider selling."

She wanted to make an appointment for four o'clock to come and see it. I could tell she was already to buy it. I hadn't even been back home for twelve hours and out of the blue somebody wanted to buy my beautiful house!

When Clyde went to the mailbox, he started visiting with our good friend John. Clyde began sharing about our trip. Clyde mentioned that we were thinking about starting a church in California.

John perked right up, "Is your place going to be for sale?" he asked.

"Yes, we'll have to sell," Clyde told him.

John asked, "How much?"

We weren't even sure at that point. So Clyde told him we'd have to get back to him on that. Clyde came up to the house and together we agreed on a price. John came over and said, "I'll pay you a thousand dollars more than your asking price."

Now in California that's common, but not in Florida, where there are hundreds of condos and homes available for sale. I could see God was visibly making it very clear that He was calling us to leave Naples.

A few hours later, our other next-door neighbor got wind of the news that we were moving and had come over to say, "I want to buy your condo." That made it three offers in six hours and we hadn't even put a For Sale sign out or even called a realtor. How clear could it be? At that moment, my heart changed about moving to California because I could see that God was definitely leading us west.

We sold the house and all its furnishings to John and his wife Irene Murphy. Once again out came the chocolate pudding and tears, knowing I had to leave what I loved for an unknown future.

But God made his direction even more clear when Clyde said, "Gerrie, I really feel that I need to talk to John and Irene about their relationship with God, before we leave."

Clyde asked John if he could talk with him about spiritual matters. John graciously accepted and asked Clyde over. Clyde dropped in and talked at length with John and Irene about what it means to have eternal life.

John and Irene both accepted the Lord Jesus into their hearts that afternoon. John told Clyde, "This is exactly what we've been looking for. We've got all the money we need, and everything we own is paid for. We have a home in Westchester, New York, and one here in Florida. But we've never really understood the Bible enough to understand that we could have eternal life."

Clyde was so thrilled. He insisted that I say good-bye to John and Irene. So the day before we left, in between my sobs, I hugged both of them good-bye and told them how happy I was they had made the decision to take Jesus into their lives.

Irene said, "Gerrie, I'm so thankful that at your ages, you and Clyde are willing to make this transition to move to Sun City. There you can help people who've acquired all their goals and don't know what to do with their lives. It's wonderful and I know God will use you there in California just like He used you to help us." Irene's words, said with such enthusiasm, made me excited to begin this new California adventure.

We were still waiting to close the final papers on the house, and with the truck all loaded, we stopped to sign the papers. The escrow officer was a young girl that I'd been working with who was fearful that she had cancer. I went through the four spiritual laws with her, and she couldn't thank me enough that she'd found the peace that she needed. It was like a closed chapter.

We signed the papers, and with the truck already loaded, this young escrow officer became the last person in Naples for us to talk to and to help find Jesus. Clyde and I drove off hand in hand waiting for the California adventure, knowing this was the perfect ending to the Naples chapter in our ministry.

Chapter 28

ON THE ROAD TO
SUN CITY

C HERIE HAD MADE up a tape of Clyde's favorite songs for us to take along on the trip to California. Traveling was slow in the car and the big van. There was such melancholy in my heart as I left behind my home, yet I knew we were responding to God's call, and I wanted to do His will.

We were driving through Arizona, not knowing what the outcome was going to be. The fears of the unknown would wash over me in waves now and then, but I would hang on to the faith that we were being sent by God.

The sun was shining brightly, through the big silvery cumulous clouds. Those rays were just bursting through the sky in glorious streaks across the sky. Clyde had Cherie's tape playing and just then the song "Day Star" came on. I do not remember the words exactly, but I do recall the message was asking the Lord to lead and promising to follow. It went on to ask God to show us new things, change wrong things into right, and for us to become a beacon of love and light for others to see God in each of us. The words to that song were our testimony, and both of us rode along with tears streaming down our faces. It was very emotional and it confirmed our commitment to the new mission.

We'd planned this big trip en route to Sacramento. It was a great chance to see the Grand Canyon. With our thin blood from Florida, we arrived at the Grand Canyon in the coldest weather on record there. They were expecting snow that day. We took one good glimpse in the cold wind.

Clyde said, "Yep, it looks just like the pictures. Let's go!" With teeth chattering we got back in the car and drove on to Sedona.

We arrived in California to a new apartment in the city of Rocklin, an upscale community about ten miles from where our new home in Lincoln Hills was being built. It was fun watching the progress of the new house.

It didn't take long for me to discover the amazingly beautiful California sunsets as I sat on the balcony of our apartment. Each night Clyde and I would sit out there to study and pray for those God would send to us as we began the new church.

As the brilliant orange and reds would wash over the Sutter Butte Mountains and I saw the purple mountain majesty of the American West, I discovered a new understanding of the lyrics to "America the Beautiful." The sky would change from orange and red to deep purple with lavender sunrays streaking across the sky. There in that masterpiece of God, Clyde and I prayed that He would send the right people to our new church and that He would allow us to attend to their spiritual needs.

This hallmark of the West was also a marvel to our grandchildren. Mark and Lori lived in Rocklin and their three children visited us every day. They too had come to love the sunsets and our prayer time and were excited for us to be starting the new church their father had inspired. We loved it when our grandchildren would remind us that the sunset was approaching, and they would come and tell us, "Grandma! Grandpa! The sun is setting. We'd better go pray."

Moving day was the first of November. We moved in and immediately Clyde went out to the new neighborhood inviting people to come to our new church. With no building, our new "Valley View Church" would meet in our home. Clyde and I were one of the first one hundred people to live in the new Del Webb retirement village, called Sun City Lincoln Hills. We started in our living room with Clyde and me and a handful of seven or eight people.

The patio of our new home faced the west, but the back fence and shrubbery blocked the view of the California sunsets I had come to treasure. Everyone in our family could see the sunset by standing by the fence, except me. I wasn't tall enough to see over the fence. That first Christmas in our new house, my grandson David gave me a decorative step stool that gave me just enough height to enjoy the view as our family continued the tradition of praying at sunset each night.

Clyde handed out new literature explaining that we would have a church in the Country Club Grand Ball Room. Clyde had secured a meeting place for us at a very nominal fee. It was a beautiful facility, with lush landscape, fountains, and even a baby grand piano. The people started coming until we grew to a congregation worshiping together on Sunday mornings.

Because we are a retirement community, we have no children in our California church. There is no Sunday school, no nursery, no youth program, and no teen events. We do not have a daily vacation Bible School in the summer. As a pastor's wife, these were often my duties and I have found this ministry has given me time to explore other ways to serve God, such as writing this book or returning to public speaking. Clyde's service is Sunday mornings only. There are no Sunday evening services and no Wednesday night service either. We encourage small groups, and without a doubt this is the smoothest ministry Clyde and I have ever had.

People have been accepting the Lord frequently in California. A lot of the people that have come to our church have had a church background in various denominations. Many of these people came with open hearts, open minds, and being out of their old environment it made it easier for them to feel comfortable with Clyde's teaching style. As Clyde explained how to have eternal life, people would begin to respond. They were eager to learn more about what the Bible had to say about how they should live their lives.

Living in California brought great joy with being so close to the grandchildren. Shortly after we moved to California, Tim accepted a call to Northern California as well. Our son Andy lived in San Diego, so suddenly we had all but Mike's children within reach.

We spent every holiday together with Tim and Michelle and Lori and Mark's families. Clyde and I made sure that we saw the children every day. We never took a day for granted. The grandchildren were in and out of the house as a natural thing. There wasn't much distinction between homes, except at bedtime when we'd all retire to our own homes. California wasn't a big adjustment, except for missing the beach and the special friends we'd left behind.

One time we went to a special get together for all the Wesleyan pastors in the Sacramento area. It was our first time to go to something like that, since we were not Wesleyan background. Another couple was there, J.R. and Linda. Clyde was really enjoying talking to J.R. out on the patio. I was chatting with Linda inside the home. Out of all the fifty or sixty people there, those happen to be the two we selected to get acquainted with. In talking with J.R. Clyde learned that J.R. had been a pastor at a couple of churches and had been very hurt. He was no longer in the ministry. Clyde found that J.R. loved to golf, but was also a musician. Clyde asked J.R., "Do you sing?"

J.R. looked at Clyde curiously, "Yes, I sing. I play the guitar when I sing."

Back in the kitchen I was talking with Linda and she was relating the same thing that J.R. was talking to Clyde about. I found out that Linda was a pianist.

Clyde told J.R., "Come and play for us some Sunday and I'll take you to golf at the new golf course in Lincoln Hills."

Linda and J.R. came to worship that next Sunday, and stayed with us for the next five years. J.R. and Linda had incredible talent and drove about sixty miles each Sunday to bring their music to our church, blessing our congregation with such joy. Then, J.R. cut a C.D. and it became very popular. Eventually they moved to a city more than one hundred miles away where they continued their music ministry.

So once again we were a congregation without music. We tried several avenues, but nothing really clicked in our hearts. Then one day in 2005, Phyllis Miller was meeting with Lori for a business reference. She started sharing her life challenges and said that due to the deaths of several close family members and finally her father, she felt lead to share her music with seniors.

With Lori's encouragement, Phylis explored our church web site, and then came to visit. She arrived just when the service was ending. I met Phylis and her husband Jim, and I invited them to lunch. Phylis offered to help us out when Clyde and I asked if she could come back to play piano for prelude and postlude of the services. We didn't have a job description, Clyde and I just signed her up.

Later, Phylis gave a testimony that her hurt was deep. She told us that the first year of her participation of Valley View, she was still angry and grieving through a plaster smile. It was hard for her to accept that our people at Valley View loved her. But the Lord began to show Phylis, who came from a charismatic background, that despite the different denominational backgrounds, her participation at Valley View was God's will. She testified that she had always been at Valley View with a big fake smile, but now it was real. She credited me with never giving up on supporting her.

This was another situation of people who were qualified for the ministry but were so hurt in trying to serve. God used Clyde and me to help Phylis to heal, and return her talents to serve again.

It took me awhile to replace my view of the ocean with my view of the mountains, but soon I came to love California. The culture was certainly different. In California I found people far more liberal and open-minded than I had experienced before, which sometimes proved more challenging than I expected. The city of Lincoln is now the fastest growing community in California and there is more here than I could have ever wanted.

Chapter 29

WHAT'S MINISTRY
WITHOUT A NOSH?

J EWISH GIRLS ALWAYS enjoy meeting one another. In California it was no different than anywhere else. One day while I was at the gym, Sandy Kline introduced herself. She asked if I was new to the community and where I was from. Within a few minutes of chatting, Sandy suspected that I was Jewish. When I confirmed that I was, I asked, "How could you tell?"

Sandy laughed, "Who else would wear diamond earrings to work out at the gym?" Sandy also asked, "Do you play Mahjong?" When I told her no, she scoffed playfully, "So how can you be Jewish?"

We went out for lunch that day eating and talking and since that day we have been on every fad new diet together that comes out. We *nosh* as we read the newest trends and have developed a wonderful friendship.

Another favorite Jewish girl here in my California home is Sylvia Studin, who knows my children love traditional Jewish foods. She often surprises us with chopped liver, matzo ball soup, and Jewish coffee cake. It's fun to interact with Jewish culture and I was thrilled to be invited to both Sandy and Sylvia's Bat Mitzvahs.

When Clyde came home one day to announce that he'd met another Messianic believer in our neighborhood, I made it a point to drop by the home of Anna Tonkin that afternoon. I discovered that Anna had been looking for a Christian church home where she could feel connected. I, of course, invited her to worship with us at the Club House in Sun City. There was a kinship immediately between us. Here we were, two Jewish girls who recognized Jesus as the promised Messiah, she just starting out in her faith, and I having lived a lifetime of faith. It was exciting for me, for there are so few Messianic believers in our community.

Anna tells her story this way:

> When I met Gerrie I knew immediately my life was going to be different. I grew up as a lonely child of privilege. The only goals I could see in life were to create wealth and to pursue wealth. My relationship with my family centered around *how no matter what*, I could never be thin enough, smart enough, or any *enough* to measure up to my parents' expectations.
>
> We attended the largest conservative Jewish reformed temple in Sacramento. My family was very involved there and supported the temple financially. My great uncle raised one million dollars for the Harry Tonkin Chapel. Basically, I was a Jewish princess, showered with material wealth, but very unhappy. My father was a very successful business owner and my mother was a socialite; I was raised by a housekeeper.
>
> I spent most of my young adult life looking for love in all the wrong places. I was a rebellious teen and I abused both alcohol and drugs. I spent fifteen years of my early adult life in a long-term relationship with a married man. I had just become a Christian

when I met and married Bill, who was also a Christian, but divorced him within three years. Bill and I were making an attempt to reestablish our relationship when I met Gerrie.

Gerrie is a shopper, a schmoozer, and a wheeler-dealer. She's a sophisticated socialite, but Gerrie has used her skills to help build the church instead of a personal empire. She is the person who doesn't watch life go by—she's the person who makes things happen. With our Jewish backgrounds, we clicked immediately and a warm, deep friendship sparked. Gerrie brought me into the church where I discovered I was accepted just as I am. Gerrie was the first Jew I met who was also a Christian. As we became acquainted, I discovered that she and I shared a great heritage, for she loves the Jewish culture as much as I do.

Gerrie was the beginning of a door opening with sunshine. Little by little the door has opened and she has brought such joy into my life and my husband's life. It was with Gerrie and Clyde's counsel that Bill and I rebuilt our shattered marriage and Clyde remarried us.

Gerrie has a compassion that warms the hearts of everyone around her. She is extremely high energy and she inspires me to use my talents for the Lord whenever she asks. Since I met Gerrie, I've gotten so close to God that my life has become full and rich. I believe that Gerrie was a piece of a puzzle that I needed to grow as a Messianic believer.

Chapter 30

REED AND FIZZY

SHORTLY AFTER WE moved to California our oldest son Mike and his wife Ellen had a their very first son and named him Reed. The family was shocked to learn that Reed was born with Melanoma. This precious little boy had to suffer through several major operations. When Reed was about to go in for his first surgery, we held a special prayer meeting at our house to pray for him. Everyone in the group got down on their knees and prayed for a miracle.

I had just met a new woman in Lincoln Hills named Fizzy, and she had been invited to attend that night. Fizzy celebrated with us when Reed's operation was extremely successful and the diagnosis came back that his condition was non-malignant. We had our miracle, and together our church family thanked God for answering our prayers. When Reed was going to have all the bandages removed, Clyde and I wanted so much to be there, and to take Reed to Disneyland to celebrate. But with a new church, and a new mortgage, money was just too tight.

My new friend Fizzy who really didn't feel too new at the time because we had bonded immediately, came up to me at a Bible study one day.

Fizzy said, "I've had a Holy nudge. I want Reed to experience Disney and I want to help." Fizzy made it financially possible for Reed's whole family to go to Disneyland. Mike, Ellen, and the kids had the time of their lives at Disneyland. God blessed them with Fizzy's generous heart for that magical trip.

I soon learned that when God nudges Fizzy, great things happen. She is an earthly angel, quietly observing and listening to the needs of others, and uses her resources to help. It's never done on impulse, but after prayerful consideration and evaluation.

Chapter 31

THANKS FOR
THE MEMORIES

ONE OF THE most difficult days of my life was learning that Clyde had suffered a heart attack while I was away at a Christian women's conference. Jill Briscoe, my favorite Christian author, was scheduled to speak, so she and a friend and I flew down from Sacramento to San Diego for the conference.

Clyde was the last person I expected to have a heart condition. He exercised daily, ate right, and was the heartiest person I knew. But he loved hamburgers and milk shakes daily.

It was on a Friday morning when Clyde drove himself to the hospital. He'd awakened with a sharp pain in the middle of his back and it soon moved around to his chest. I was in San Diego, so without me to consult, he thought he'd get a professional opinion.

Clyde waited in the emergency room for about twenty anxious minutes when they took an electrocardiogram (EKG) only to discover that he was having a significant heart attack. Clyde called Tim while he was waiting in the lobby to let him know that he was there, and Tim called our daughter

Lori and both of them arrived at the hospital to wait with Clyde.

As God would have it, while I was attending the conference in San Diego, our son Mike was visiting with our son Andy who lived in San Diego. Tim and Lori huddled up on her cell phone to do a three-way call to include all four of my children. In the crisis, they were concerned about their father, but also desperate to protect me from the pain that might be ahead. Together they prayed for Clyde's recovery and for wisdom in telling me what had happened.

The conference was wonderful and as one of the speakers was finishing her talk, I thought I'd avoid the crowds by sneaking out early to use the restroom. I was surprised when I saw Andy standing in the foyer of the entrance of the convention center. I thought, "Why is he here so early?"

I knew we were going out for dinner that night, but it was way too early for dinner. I ran up to him and said, "Hi Andy." I looked at his face and I knew something wasn't right.

Andy spoke softly, "Come on Mom, we need to leave right now."

I looked at him and shook my head, "I can't leave now, my friend Sally is here. I can't just desert her."

Andy was insistent, "Mom, we have to go now."

Fearfully, I looked into Andy's eyes and asked, "Why? Is something wrong?"

Andy looked at me and tears filled his eyes.

I said, "Is it Clyde?"

Andy nodded and quietly said, "Yes, Mom. He's having a heart attack."

Before I could even react, Andy went on to say, "I've got all the arrangements made for us to fly to Sacramento immediately. Let's go!"

I just stood there, trying to take it all in. I said to Andy, "What am I going to do about Jill?"

Andy, my son, the police sergeant, the best trained for a crisis, replied, "I'll handle it." He went into the auditorium to find Jill. Fortunately Jill wasn't speaking at that time and Andy located her and they came out of the auditorium. Jill said they would immediately pray for Clyde, and told me, "Gerrie, just go, I'll get home okay by myself."

This was the biggest thing I'd ever been faced with. I don't know if I just thought Clyde and I were going to live on together forever, but a heart attack was the last thing I expected. Clyde was the utmost in physical fitness. He was one of the better softball payers in Sun City and in Naples his team had won four tournaments.

He wasn't your average person, and now he was lying in a hospital in a critical care unit. We rushed to the airport, only to be delayed due to the fog at the Sacramento airport. Andy, Mike, and I prayed with a beautiful and compassionate Christian woman we had just met in the airport. The boarding announcement came within five minutes.

Back in Sacramento, Clyde had been transferred from the emergency room to the ICU and the staff worked diligently to get him stabilized. Tim and Lori were able to stay with him the entire time. Clyde led the prayers, and as he prayed he asked God for His perfect will. I don't remember the ride to the airport. I got to the hospital and was shocked at all the tubes attached to Clyde and the gray, gray skin of my usually tanned and vital husband.

I was just so thankful to be together with Clyde; that was all I could think about. I knew that I had to remain strong and I just entrusted the care and recovery of Clyde to the Lord. I knew that in all the challenges the Lord gave me, this was the one I had been being prepared for. "I must be strong," I thought.

I had no idea how severe and serious things were, until after Clyde's surgery. But because Clyde has been so disciplined in the Lord all these years, he became disciplined in doing exactly what the doctor told him to in recovery with his eating habits and exercise.

The children all gathered around the hospital bed with me, as Clyde shared with us some thoughts that once again challenged our faith. With a peace that passes all understanding, Clyde shared that although he felt that all would be fine, he needed to say a few things, just in case the Lord were to call him home. Clyde shared how thankful he was for our family; and so comforted to know that all who are old enough to understand have accepted Jesus as Savior; and is proud of the paths our children had chosen.

He challenged each of them to continue to live to please the Lord and to share His good news. As his voice broke, he insisted that no matter whether his funeral was in a few days or in a few years, he wanted very little emphasis on him and to focus that event on the Lord Jesus Christ, who truly deserves it.

Clyde had heart surgery and made a full recovery. Two years later, we celebrated our fiftieth anniversary. The entire family was present, and our church celebrated with us. The highlight of the occasion was the song that Clyde wrote and sang to me to the tune of Bob Hope's version of "Thanks for the Memories":

Thanks Gerrie, for the memories
We met on a double date,
But you were with the other mate
It all took place in Kalamazoo
Where we said bye bye to the other two
Oh we did that my dear

Oh thanks Gerrie, for the memories
"Three Coins in the Fountain" was our song
In a courtship that wasn't all that long
As your family told you tell me good bye
Instead we thought we'd give it a try
We were crazy, my dear.

Thanks Gerrie, for the memories
Can still see your tears in that bandana
As we did the unthinkable
Eloping to Angola, Indiana
Both families thought it would never last
But fifty years later, we're still having a blast
We fooled them, my dear!

Oh God gave us four wonderful young ones
Our beautiful daughter and three handsome hardy
    sons
Later all marrying spouses so right of them
Giving us twelve grandchildren, each a perfect gem

Oh, thanks for the memories
Like many trips over to the Holy Land
Seeing Galilee, Jericho, Jerusalem, Oh how grand
Or vacationing with family at Lake Michigan
Memories cherished, like this day, once again
I'm grateful my dear

Then God lead us here to Sun City
Where if you can't find friends, you're a pity
Pastoring Valley View has been a total delight
With God sending people that seem oh so right
Yes, thanks for the memories.

Without you life would have been dull
Like driving my car on the golf course what gall
Yet, through these fifty years all the bargaining you've
    made
Without you my dear, extra money would have paid
Oh thank you Gerrie dear.

So thanks for sharing your life with me
While I sold meat or manufactured shoes or ministry
Pulling together and following the Lord's sure way
For all of our family it did eternally pay

So thanks for all the memories!
I'm grateful for what together we've been through
There's not much I'd want to rearrange
I know, maybe one more Great Dane for a change
Oh Gerrie, I love you!

I'm thankful that people look at the relationship between
Clyde and me as a continuing love affair. I'm happy that our
love is not ordinary. After fifty-three years, I still get excited
when I see his car drive in the driveway. And he's the first
person I want to share any news with. He loves it when I say,
"Have I got something to tell you!" He's my soul mate, my
partner, and my best friend.

This is not to suggest that we never disagree. We might
banter back and forth some, but today, there are no fights;
just tiffs that blow over quickly and in laughter. Our years

together, and the challenges that we have faced, have allowed us to grow together and learn from them.

One of our biggest challenges today is that we share an office and his chair is only three feet from mine. We share a telephone line and a computer, which often conflict with our individual study styles. Yet, we laugh at this as trivial, for it's been almost eight years that we've been doing this, with minimal conflicts.

California has become home and a favorite ministry. I am so thankful that Clyde and I are able to continue serving the Lord in our senior years. The youthfulness and vitality of our lives is enriched with the active faith. Our people are so supportive and appreciative.

~

Joan and I sat next to each other at a tap dance luncheon. I wanted to keep staring at her because her smile was so engaging. During our conversation, we discovered we were both Jewish. I explained to her I was also a Christian, a pastor's wife. She told her husband about our meeting and all about me. She said, "Lee, you'll absolutely love her." He looked at Joan, stretched out his hand, put two thumbs down, and said, "I won't like her."

Not knowing he wouldn't like me, I put their names on the guest list for our fiftieth anniversary celebration. On the way home that night, Joan asked Lee if he had changed his mind. He answered, "I don't like her—I love her." Today, Lee and Joan are involved with Christians United for Israel and even had us over for dinner with their Rabbi. What a special friendship.

Chapter 32

OUR CHILDREN

ROM THE TIME our children were small, Clyde and I prayed for their future spouses. We prayed that God would guide the children to find just the right person to compliment each of their personalities and to be a supporting life mate. Ellen, Cathy, Mark, and Michelle have clearly been the perfect choices for each of our children. As I observe how they have melted their lives together as one, and raised their children to love the Lord, what more could I ask for?

Clyde and I are the proud grandparents of a dozen grandchildren: Steffenie, Andrea, Rachel, David, Nathan, Jonathon, Aubrie, Aundrea, Alexa, Reed, Caroline, and Wilson.

Mike is our oldest son. He was called to the ministry at age twelve and it was clear to all that Mike was divinely inspired. A national weekly Christian publication called *Teen Power* featured a photo of Mike and his testimony when he was about thirteen. Young people were encouraged to send their testimony to this publication.

Mike met his wife Ellen through our daughter Lori. Ellen and Lori were roommates at Taylor University. Years later, Ellen was with me when I was sorting through some old papers. I pulled out a copy of the *Teen Power* article featuring Mike from ten years before.

Ellen gasped! "I know that photo!" she exclaimed. "I read that article as a young girl and promised my friends that I would marry someone just like that!" Ellen's eyes danced as she realized that God had been fashioning a plan for her life way back then.

Mike is the pastor of Northridge Church in southern New Hampshire, a booming, contemporary church where Mike and Ellen are reaching out to the surrounding communities.

Mike recalls his youth like this:

> There was always a sense of joy growing up in our household. Laughter was always just a moment away. Both Mom and Dad gave us Mills kids the gift of laughter and a happy home. Whenever I think back on my childhood and to this day when I picture my mother in my mind she is smiling, her Jewish eyes twinkling, and her laughter contagious.
>
> Whenever mom came home from shopping or running errands we all knew one of two things just happened; that she'd gotten the most unbelievable deal shopping and she'd had an opportunity to share her faith. It was and still is a way of life for her, and I learned from the best the joy of doing both effectively.
>
> I remember lying in bed at night hearing my mom and dad pray together out loud in their bedroom before they went to sleep. It was tremendous source of comfort.
>
> Mom and Dad always had an open door policy at our home. Anyone from the church could stop by at any time and were made to feel welcome. If it was dinnertime Mom would insist whoever stopped by, pull up a chair at the kitchen table and join us. It taught me a lot about how to have a servant's heart as a preacher.

Christmastime was always special because we knew that mom grew up Jewish and missed out on celebrating Christmas in her childhood and was making up for it with us.

She turned our house into the most dazzling Christmas display that made the holidays feel extra special. And despite the warnings each Christmas not to expect too many presents this year, Mom and Dad always figured out a way on a pastor's salary to fill the room around and under the Christmas tree with presents.

Dad always made us aware of how special we were that our mother was Jewish. Every new Bible story we learned taught us even more about our Jewish heritage. Growing up half Jewish, knowing that I could be related to King David, the David who killed Goliath, actually gave me confidence as a kid.

I learned from Mom how to be both passionate about my faith in Christ and my Jewish heritage at the same time. That one didn't take away from the other and in fact it made it even more special.

Mom wasn't a big sports fan but she was when it came to watching her children participate in sports. She attended every game, sitting along with Dad in the bleachers cheering us without fully understanding the sport we were playing. I remember in seventh grade basketball, she jumped to her feet and was cheering me on as I stole the ball from my opponent and dribbled in all alone for the score toward the other team's basket!

I had gone the wrong way and neither Mom nor I knew it until we heard the screams from my coach and teammates. Mom didn't care if I'd scored for the wrong team. I scored and that's what mattered. She jumped up and yelled, "Yeah Mike! Way to go! That's my boy!"

I always admired my mother's bargaining ability and how it was just part of her personality. From the time the sun rose every day, it was a given, Mom would enjoy people, period. Somehow we knew she could enjoy them even more if she could charm them into a better deal. We knew that whether it was a restaurant or an amusement park; a furniture store or even a grocery store if Mom turned on the charm, the spell was cast and it was just a matter of time and a good deal would be struck. I remember that she once walked out of a store with thirteen frozen pies just because the crust was cracked. Such a deal!

Growing up a "preacher's kid" meant the church was the focal point of my life. Mom and Dad never had to drag us kids to church. First of all we knew it was expected of us and there wasn't an option. But most important, they made church to be balanced, joyful, and worshipful and that's where all of our friendships centered. Some preacher's kids felt funny about being a "PK." I loved knowing that my dad and my mom were called by God.

Our second son is Andy, serves as a Police Lieutenant in San Diego in charge of the Gang Unit. Andy recalls his childhood warmly:

The main recollection I have about growing up is that Mom and Dad were always around. We didn't have to wonder whether we would see our parents that day. Dad began his workday early so that he would be available for all our ball games or after school events. Amazingly, with all the sports I played, my dad only missed one game in my life, and that was a college game, while he was in Israel and couldn't get back in time.

Being a "Preacher's kid" had both good and bad sides. It afforded Mom and Dad the opportunity to be with the family more on a consistent basis. But in some ways the lack of privacy or expectation that our family was held to a different standard challenged me. In spite of not having an abundance of money, Mom made me feel special. When she went to the store she brought one of us kids home a special (cheap) treat. Something we really liked. Even if it wasn't our favorite, she said it with such conviction it became our favorite.

But there were great advantages, too, like being able to play basketball at one o'clock in the morning with all the guys at the church. Rubber court, glass backboards, and electronic scoreboard—life was good.

Mom taught me to be professional. She taught me to be positive, to speak well, and to articulate my thoughts with conviction. She'd encourage me daily, by saying things like, "Andy, you're so bright, and you have the ability to mix and appreciate people at all levels."

By example she taught me to not be judgmental and to appreciate the gifts of others. Her support and encouragement gave me confidence to walk in front of large groups and be proud of what I am, recognizing that it's a culmination of my upbringing and the gifts God has blessed me with.

These were powerful lessons, which proved extremely valuable as my career lead me all over the world speaking to government leaders, law enforcement officials, and political dignitaries.

I grew up so proud of being Jewish that I had an Israeli flag in my room and was prepared to join the

Israeli army. Since we lived where there we no other Jews, I learned how to be Jewish from Mom and my grandparents. One of my friends once told me, "Man, Andy, your mom looks like Barbra Streisand." It made me proud of her.

I learned to love my heritage and explored it with books like Exodus. I even learned some Hebrew on my own. In Israel I found it fascinating to walk where Jesus walked, to see the rich history of God's people, and recognized His greater plan for mankind.

My siblings and I share a great history. Tim, Lori, and I went to Florida Bible College all at the same time. Tim and I were roommates and as the oldest, I thought I'd set a good example and help him to get a good start and be really focused at this new school. I told him, "Hey look, all these other guys are going to be looking for girls this first week. Let's you and I agree to buckle down and not even talk to any girls for a while. Then, in a in a month or so we'll start looking around."

Tim thought a minute and then said, "Good idea!" Younger brothers are always naive. We shook hands, and I walked out of our dorm room and there in the hall I spotted Cathy. I turned around and went back into the room and told Tim, "Deal's off!" A year later, Cathy and I were married. We now have three beautiful girls who love God and their grandparents.

After about two years of service in the ministry, Andy felt God call him to return to full-time police work. Cathy is from San Diego and Andy chose to take a job with the San Diego Police Department. He is now a lieutenant in charge of the San Diego Gang Unit. Andy helped transition the police department to community policing.

He has been decorated with many prestigious honors including the Herman Goldstein Awards for Excellence in Problem Oriented Policing and finished as a finalist in three others. These awards are handed out each year for global recognition of excellence in problem solving. Andy received this award in recognition of his project Operation Hot Pipe and Smoke Haze. They tackled a drug trafficking problem in neighborhoods where gang members had controlled areas for profit.

Early in President Bill Clinton's administration, Andy flew to New York to help him announce the Crime Bill. That legislation was the hallmark of the Clinton Administration. Andy appeared on all the major TV networks with the President, and I switched channels all day and all night to see them all as they were repeated.

It was in Washington DC where Andy received the Gary P. Hayes Award, which is given by major city police chiefs to the police person who has lead the country in law enforcement innovation. This is the highest award given in law enforcement by the Police Executive Research Forum.

To Andy though, the most prestigious award he received was a plaque from his patrol officers. It reads, "To a true leader and fellow warrior." Andy tells me that this award means more to him than all of the others.

I recall after months of persuasion, Andy finally agreed to take me on a "ride along" with him. I was so proud of my son the cop, and I eagerly anticipated action. In fact, I even prayed for action that day. Andy had taken the guys in the family out, but he would never take me. He finally agreed that I could go, but only in the daytime when it was safer. He made me dress in dark clothing, and I practiced the cop walk, with my tough look. It's kind of hard for a five-foot-two, one hundred-twenty-pound Jewish girl from Kalamazoo to look tough. I passed the swagger inspection, with Andy laughing at my "tough" demeanor.

I got in the patrol car, finally on my first police venture. It seemed too quiet when all of a sudden, over the radio came, "211 (Robbery) now at the B of A, 5700 ECB. Beep. Beep. Beep. 211 now, B of A, 5700 ECB." The lights went on. Andy asked me if I was frightened.

I shook my head. "Never admit fear," I was told. We drove right to the bank and Andy blocked in a car with his patrol car. How did he know which car to block? They didn't' tell me. He came out with the robber, spread him across the car. When Andy had the man secured, he let me get out of the car.

I whispered to Andy, "He's crying."

"He should be," was the reply.

I touched Andy's shoulder, "But, Andy," I said sadly, "That's somebody's son."

Andy gave me a look that indicated that he was not too concerned. As it turned out the teller overreacted and it wasn't really a robbery. The bandit was just trying to pass stolen and forged checks at the bank.

So after that guy was apprehended, Andy took care of a routine drug dealer. Over the radio I heard, "We have the warrant to search," with a scratching location mumbled after.

"Hold on, Mom," Andy warned me. "Here we go." The sirens came back on, and there I was flying through the streets of San Diego with my son the cop! It was exhilarating!

As we raced through red lights and darted around parked

cars, Andy told me, "When I get out of the car, you get right behind me. Every step I take, you take."

I nodded and when the car screeched to a halt, Andy jumped out. I was right behind him. With gun drawn he pounded on the door. A little man came and asked, "What's the problem?" through sleepy eyes.

Andy growled, "You know what the problem is."

The guy scratched his head, "Why I don't know, what do you mean?" He was a cute little guy and his hair was all mussed up like he'd just gotten out of bed.

Andy told him. "We have a warrant to search your home."

He nodded and stepped aside. Andy walked into the house and I walked right behind him. Still pointing his gun, Andy demanded, "Where's your wife?"

The man said, "Working."

The rest of Andy's team started searching house. Andy stood tall, demanding more information. "What kind of car does she drive?"

The man answered, "A Volvo."

Andy wasn't satisfied, "What color?"

"Red," he answered looking away.

Andy's eyes squinted just a bit, "Why is there a red Volvo parked down the street?" he demanded.

I thought, "What red Volvo? How could Andy notice a specific car at the rate of speed we were approaching this house?"

The little man was getting nervous. "Maybe she had a problem and took the bus to work," he replied.

Andy's eyes were steel. "Uh huh," was all he said.

Andy had barely gotten that statement out, when the rest

of the team found the drugs. They were hidden in the tubes in the TV.

Then I found out this was the man's third strike. This charge would send him to prison for life. He was handcuffed and loaded into another cruiser and taken to jail.

What I loved the most about that day was watching Andy in his calling. There were children downstairs, whimpering, and petrified that Mommy's boyfriend, (not husband) was going away with the policeman. They didn't understand why all the police were surrounding their house.

As the team packed up after the arrest, Andy got on one knee with the children. Andy began to talk to the children and as kind as he is, even though he's a tough cop, he explained to the children that their mommy had been called and she'd be home soon.

In a gentle voice, Andy smiled at them. "We are not going to leave you alone. One of your neighbors will take care of you until she gets there," he told them.

My son the cop, tough, but tender, had shown me a fresh appreciation for his work in the city of San Diego.

⁓

Our daughter Lori and her husband Mark pastor a church in El Dorado Hills, California, called Bridgepointe. Lori remembers her child with deep fondness:

> As I grew up, I remember so much passion and peace in our home. Dad's faith and dedication to the Lord brought such stability and Mom's passion and vibrancy made it so exciting. Mom is passionate about everything! Whether she is painting, shopping for the right outfit, decorating the house, fixing the food, counseling,

or just talking to someone one the phone, whatever she does, she gives it 150 percent. She is inspiring in all that she does. Mom has always risen early and is still going strong at midnight, working hard and helping others. I admire her and I get the biggest kick out of just watching her operate. Often, my dad leans over and whispers in my ear, with an adoring smirk on his face and tears in his eyes... Isn't she somethin'?" He's so right. She is somethin' and I'm grateful that she's *my* mom and *my* best girlfriend!

Mom and Dad modeled the most beautiful marriage to not only my brothers and me, but to all the people around them. While growing up I had friends often say to me that they would give anything to have parents like mine and a family like ours. Oh how blessed I feel to have been raised with so much love, passion, fun and faith. My parents really loved and adored each other and were committed to their kids, providing us with the best start in life imaginable.

Mom and Dad have always been very affectionate. I love "the look" when their favorite song, "Three Coins in the Fountain" comes on the radio! It's as if the world stops spinning for a brief moment! I wish I had a dime for all of the times I've seen Dad spontaneously walk up to Mom and give her the most loving touch or romantic kiss while she is standing over the stove fixing dinner. She melts faster than the butter! Their love for each other has been such a great example and a one that I learned first hand what I was looking for in my own marriage and what I was eventually blessed with. According to my brothers, my husband, Mark has earned the birthright of our family. Together, Mark and I have been blessed with three amazing sons.

Mom and Dad also modeled how to deal with difficult situations with simple faith. When I was very young and impressionable, Mom and Dad had suffered a pretty tough attack by parishioners. I woke up about 2 a.m. to their voices murmuring in prayer. I could see their silhouettes against the window. They were both on their knees next to their bed, praying for love and understanding for the very people who were attacking them. That was a pivotal moment of spiritual development in my life. After getting past the anger towards those who were hurting them, their faith brought me to tears of humility and challenged me to be just as forgiving as they were. It was a lesson I have tried to emulate ever since then and it is a lesson that is much better caught than taught!

Spiritually I was so challenged by the way Mom and Dad modeled how to walk with Christ, how to talk to people about him and live a life to honor him. They showed us how to pray about everything and we'd watch them consistently reading their Bibles. It was such a comfort as a teenager, to stumble out of my bedroom (long after they were up and out). I'd walk down the hallway to see Mom's little worn spot on the sofa, where she had her quiet time everyday. I smiled to see her Bible sitting on the coffee table and her glasses on top. I knew she'd been up early that morning, having her quiet time with God, praying for me and the rest of the family and the issues of the day. She has always been committed to supporting whatever her children were facing in prayer with her whole heart. Whatever it was, Mom owned it in prayer as if it were her own issue. Even today if I confide in her, I know she immediately turns it over to the Lord.

When my husband and I were preparing to move from Canada back to the United States (which Mom had been longing and praying hard for), we were trying to sell our house. We had a well and the water report came back contaminated, putting the sale of our home at risk. I called Mom, our little prayer warrior, and she prayed fervently as she always does for God to help us. When the next day when she was praying and reading the bible, she read in 1 Kings how "the water was healed" she knew that it was a special little message from the Lord.

Mom picked up the phone, called, and said, "Worry no more." I was just reassured that everything would be all right and sure enough it was!

Growing up with Jewish traditions mixed with the Christian faith, especially being a pastor's kid, made for a life full of fun and faith, all intertwined. I couldn't tell where one began and the other one ended. All I know is that is gave me the most incredible beginning a kid could possibly have, and I always felt "special." What a heritage!

We've never really celebrated the religious holidays, but we've always celebrated being *Jewish.* I was very close to my Jewish grandparents and my Aunt Bedonna. I have such precious memories with them. It was neat growing up with my Yiddish speaking great-grandfather who lived with my grandparents. We weren't able to talk much to him because of the language barrier...but we communicated very well! The love was strong. We were taught to appreciate the sacrifices he made, leaving the country he knew and loved, to provide such a great and free life for his family.

What a privilege to be Clyde and Gerrie's daughter! What a joy it was to be a pastor's kid! What a blessing it is to be a Christian! What an honor to be half Jewish! I have always felt like the "Chosen One."

~

Our youngest son Tim pastors a new church planted in the same community where Clyde and I live called The Ridge. He considers his parents his best friends. Tim remembers his childhood this way:

> Growing up in our house was always a kick. Mom had so much energy and it inspired everyone around her. There was a lot of love in our house, and just as much laughter. It was fun being the youngest in the family, because they all looked out for me.
>
> I never wondered what was expected of me, growing up because Mom and Dad made it clear every day. They taught us to love God and to serve him with all that we did. I remember riding on the homecoming float in high school, when I had to make a decision about teen drinking. The kids all knew that I was a non-drinker, but the peer pressure was on for me to drink that night. Even though I didn't condemn those kids for drinking, they didn't respect me for my choice not to drink.
>
> It was tough to jump down off that float and walk home, choosing not to be part of a teen beer party. The taunts and jeers about being "too good for them," or "the preacher's kid" hurt, but I knew it was the right thing to do because I knew what my parents expected of me. It wasn't easy, but I could do it because of the way they had instructed me. Mom and Dad had taught me that leaders are made from responsible choices

and God blesses responsible leaders. If Mom and Dad had not demonstrated that being a Christian is fun, exciting, unpredictable and choice driven, I might not have begun my calling as a Christian leader. That night I developed character and knew I had the courage to answer a call from God.

Being Jewish is the finest gift my mother ever gave me. Knowing my Jewish grandparents and learning to appreciate the Jewish culture has enriched my life in many ways. We celebrated Hanukah and eight days of presents were a great prelude to Christmas. Out of the four kids, they all say I'm the most Jewish. Physically I resemble more of my mom's side than the other siblings. When I officiated at my grandmother's funeral the relatives bragged that I looked more like the Rabbi than the real Rabbi did.

Mom and Dad never made much money but as kids, we never knew we were poor. I thought I was the richest kid in America. Mom and Dad saved for fantastic Christmases and vacations. We were surrounded by families with wealth, but the power of family was greater than the power of money. Mom used to go to the store and by Ideal cookies, Fortified Oak Flakes and Mountain Dew. She'd unpack the groceries and within fifteen minutes they were all gone. She'd pretend to be mad and say, "Never am I doing that again! Never!" but she always did. Our house always had kids in the church over at all times of day and night. We were always out of milk, brownies, and cookies because as fast as she could put them on the table, they were gone.

Mom and Dad are the finest parents I've ever met. They taught three things which were critical to my success. The first is to walk in Christ; to trust him in all facets of my life. The second is discipline. Mom and Dad demonstrated that love, fun, and discipline all worked together. Dad was a man who stuck to his word. He agreed with Joshua, "as for me and my family, we will serve the LORD" (24:15). There were no options, no bartering; this was his law and it was laid in love. And the third thing Mom and Dad taught me was how to have a blast as a Christian. Dad was willing to allow me to go twenty-four hours away to Bible college, when I couldn't enjoy the Bible college just two hours away. He taught me that living Christian life is the most fun you can do.

I have followed my parents' ministry wherever they have gone because my parents are my best friends. Today they live within walking distance of my home. If they accepted a new call, I probably would too, and we'd probably end up within three miles of each other again.

My wife Michelle, shares these same feelings. One year Michelle hand wrote my mother a Mother's Day card that quoted the Book of Ruth 1:16, "Wherever you go, I will go; wherever you live, I will live. Your people will be my people, and your God will be my God."

That's the kind of relationship Michelle and my mom have. Mom, Lori, and Michelle are inseparable. They are all pastors' wives and this creates a bond that supports each of them in their life challenges. Most days I think Mom likes Michelle better than me.

～

My grandson David has developed a special passion for his Jewish heritage. He tells about his memories this way:

I've always had a confidence in my life because of my grandparents. While other Jewish grandmothers are

pushing baby strollers around introducing the grand-
child as a doctor or lawyer, my grandma introduced
me to everyone as, "This is my grandson David, and
he's such a good boy." How could I ever let her down?
The legacy she's instilled of confidence is carried out in
my ability to perform in music or theatre, my ability to
negotiate a contract, to develop a friendship, even in
money making.

Grandma would always make fun things for us.
Once she told us we were going to have biscuits and
gravy, but she put chocolate pudding over the biscuits
instead of gravy. She put marshmallows in macaroni
and cheese, just to hear us laugh. When she would visit
us in Canada, Grandma would have to make a grand
entrance like Lucille Ball. My mom would hold the
front door shut and say, "David! Guess who's here?"

Then Grandma would open the door and she'd say
in her funny Jewish voice, "It's *Grandma!*" and I would
run into her arms.

Grandma was proud of my acting ability, which
has driven me to perform. The two best performances
of my life were the two nights that my Grandma flew
in from California to Indiana Wesleyan University to
see me as the Major General Stanley in the *Pirates of
Penzance*.

I pulled out all the stops, and used up all my energy
in anticipation of Grandma telling me "David, you
are the best actor I've ever seen!" I had just enough
strength left after the show to give her a hug.

One of the most significant times in my life was
when Grandma took me to Israel. I got off the airplane
and standing looking over the city, there a powerful
emotion of gratitude came over me. I remember feeling

so blessed to have five thousand years of heritage because of my grandmother. I was there with my mom and Grandma, and I understood that being Jewish is passed down through the mother. I felt so close to God and so chosen. My Grandma brought me to that. God was working in my heart, calling me that day. And since that day, I've often felt as if my heart is in Jerusalem because I left it there.

~

One time I flew up from Florida to Michigan for a speaking engagement. I stayed at Mike's house and as I prepared for the speaking event, I decided that I really wanted to look good. I booked a hair appointment at an expensive salon across town, about fifteen miles away. The morning of my appointment, a terrible ice storm hit the area. Schools were closed, roads were glazed with ice, and all news bulletins warned of the dangers of travel, asking everyone to stay off the roads. There were dozens of accidents in the area but I was still determined to have my hair styled professionally.

I asked Mike if he'd drive me. He looked at me in shock and replied calmly, "Mom, you can't even think about getting on the road today. Cars are in the ditches all over. It's far too treacherous to be out on the road today."

I wasn't impressed with the storm. I said, "Mike, I've got to go. I made this appointment weeks ago, and I really need to look my best for the conference."

Mike shook his head sadly, "Mom, it's not going to happen. I can't risk taking you out on such dangerous roads."

I pleaded, "Mike! I've got to go! I'm begging you to take me! Please."

It took awhile, but I heaped on enough Jewish guilt, tears, and threats that Mike finally brought the car around front and I climbed in for my hair appointment.

We road silently for a few miles, and I noted the ice hanging from the power lines, the glassy, frosted look of the roads, and the battered, disabled cars that looked as if they'd been strewn along the side of the road.

Mike looked at me out of the corner of his eye as we passed one corner with several cars banged up along the side of the road and said grimly, "Mom, the only people on the road now are the county road crews, emergency vehicles, the police, and one son of a Jewish mother."

~

My son Andy, the police lieutenant in charge of gang control in San Diego, was planning a trip to visit recently. I wanted to make arrangements to be at the airport when he arrived, but I didn't know what time he would be arriving. I called Andy on the telephone and got his voice mail, so I left a message instructing him to call me as soon as possible, and to let me know what time his plane would land in Sacramento.

When Andy didn't call me back right away, I called him a second time and left a similar message. But Andy still didn't call me back. I mentioned it to my youngest son, Tim, who called Andy to see what he could find out.

When Tim reached Andy in person, Andy's comment was, "Tim, tell Mom, I'm trying to break up warfare between the Crypts and the Bloods." Andy continued, "There are bullets flying all over San Diego, I'm in charge, and she's upset that I didn't call her back with flight information for next week!"

Chapter 33

DUKE, AND BIBLES
IN RUSSIA

A MILLS FAMILY HISTORY cannot be written without mention of the seven Great Danes we have owned over the years. My first encounter with the breed happened when we were back in Bible college.

When Clyde was a child, he admired his neighbor's stately Great Dane. So when we moved into our new house on Montgomery Street, Clyde could hardly wait to bring a puppy home for the children. His name was Duke and he was a fawn-colored clown with great big feet and a sloppy wet tongue. What I didn't realize was that the puppy was going to grow up to be the size of a small horse.

We kept Duke in the basement and the children loved him. I wasn't so sure. Dogs had never been part of my lifestyle and I didn't know how to take care of a puppy and I didn't really want to learn how.

When Christmas came, I was afraid that Duke would knock over our beautiful tree, so we borrowed a neighbor's playpen and put the tree in the playpen. I tossed the children's presents in there, too. I was confident that I'd secured Christmas for the children and no dog damage would befall our holiday.

Duke was in the basement when we left for church, but when we came home, we discovered that this big dopey dog had managed to escape to the living room. He had knocked the tree out of the playpen and torn up the packages as well. There were broken ornaments, and pieces of wrapping paper and ribbon all over the house. In his fun and fury, Duke had also messed all over the carpeting.

Later, when we were living in Quincy, and raising our four children next door to the church, it meant plenty of extra children in and out of the house all day long. I never knew for sure how many people to plan for at dinnertime because Clyde or one of the children would invariably ask someone to stay. We enjoyed a sort of organized confusion of fun and activity in a noisy house of children and teenagers. So when Clyde brought home another Great Dane puppy it just added to the confusion.

While Clyde was an excellent disciplinarian with the children, he was terrible at using the same philosophy with the puppy. I didn't allow the dog in the house, but the minute I left the house to run an errand, someone in the family would invite the dog inside. While other neighborhood dogs were taught to "sit" or "stay," our dog was best at messing on the carpet. The children enjoyed rough housing with the dog.

Clyde loved to take the dog to the office over at the church. I liked him over there best, too. When it came to dog psychology, I preferred the "out of sight, out of mind" philosophy.

One time while Clyde was preaching, a skunk sprayed the dog. It was summer and the windows were open. The smell came wafting through the house with the summer breeze and Clyde didn't even slow his sermon down. He kept right on preaching until he noticed that the entire congregation had eyes and noses running from the smell. The worse part was when the kids grabbed my newly canned tomatoes and poured them on the dog to extinguish the odor.

The final straw that broke this camel's back was when we had a house full of company and one of the children left the dog locked in the bedroom downstairs while we all went to a concert at church. They had forgotten that the dog was down there. When I saw Clyde try to sneak by me with Kentucky Fried Chicken buckets filled with dog manure I knew there was a major mess down there to be reckoned with.

I completely lost my temper. There was no way to tell that I was a Christian woman dedicated to the Lord. The family finally agreed that the dog might be happier in a different home. The family all knew that I'd reached my limit of Great Dane grace.

~

I have always been open and outgoing, and unafraid to talk to strangers. When we were in Bible college, and Clyde was studying for the ministry, Mr. Miles asked me if I would be willing to speak for a meeting to share my story. They were going to be speaking at an event, and invited me to join them. It was the first time I had ever shared publicly at a church.

Clyde was the one studying to be a pastor, and learning how to plan sermons and to be a good speaker. I wasn't thinking that I would have my own independent ministry. I knew that I was Clyde's partner in everything, including his ministry. But when people wanted to hear me speak, it was so unexpected and I was encouraged by the response.

The first time I spoke lead to another engagement, and from there another. What was humorous about it was that as I spoke week after week, I started traveling farther from home. Clyde would drive me, take his books along, and be my bus driver. Somebody even bought him a bus driver buckle. He was studying and I was doing the speaking.

As a Christian speaker, also recognized as a Messianic Jew (or Jewish believer), it has been my mission to share how God works in my life. I've spoken on each of the seven trips to Israel, and at Christian women's clubs all over the country.

I was able to travel over the years throughout the United States, especially many places in Michigan, Indiana, and Illinois. It was so nice to be able to travel and have it all paid for and stay in nice hotels together. Nancy, from our church in Michigan, would take care of our small children and would have food and homemade pies ready for me whenever I came back from a big speaking engagement.

~

Eventually I developed a topic that as a Jewish girl, I had finally found what I was looking for in Jesus, and that's what I began speaking on. I spoke to groups of all sizes and religious backgrounds. I spoke at churches, schools, and banquets, in large auditoriums, women's retreats, or small intimate gatherings; wherever God would have me to go.

In spring of 1994, Mark and Lori were going to Russia to conduct music for an evangelistic tour all over Russia. When the coordinator heard that Lori and I were related, he invited me to go as well. He wanted me to share my faith at the different venues on the tour. I seized the opportunity to go and when I shared with our church, one little boy came up to donate thirty-six dollars. It was all the money he had. I didn't' want to take his money and his parents didn't want him to give me everything he had. But he insisted. That was the first money that came in for the trip, and the rest arrived within a week or so.

My nine-year-old grandson David was going along to sing at the elementary schools and hospitals for the children, so he agreed to be my roommate for the trip. Our first stop was Moscow where the tour guide said to us, "Eat up at McDonalds! It will be the last American-tasting food for awhile." I soon knew what he meant, because the rest of the food I was served in Russia took a major adjustment.

We left Moscow and at our next hotel there was some kind of a central control for the heat that somehow affected the water. When David and I got to the hotel, I turned on the bath water and it came out coffee brown. The room was cold. The heat had been turned off for the day and with my thin Florida blood, it was bitterly cold for me.

I told my grandson, "David, you might want to take a bath."

David took one look at that coffee colored water and said, "Grandma, I'm not getting into that water!"

I tried to laugh it off, "Oh David, It's fine. There's nothing wrong with it, see?" and I stuck my hand in it. David made a face at the water, but agreed, and I left him to quickly bathe. It was so cold, he came running out of the bathroom wrapped in a big towel and jumped under the down comforter on his bed and I tucked it all around him.

Now it was my turn. If David could do it, I could, too. I went into the bathroom and turned on the water. It came rushing out brown as mud. I stood there, staring at it thinking, "How can I do this?"

Mustering all my will, I bathed without washing my platinum blonde hair. I knew that if I put that water on my hair, it would turn completely brown or orange. What was I going to do? I had to speak here for the next two weeks.

I sat down and prayed on the edge of the tub, "Lord, I'm going to be here for two weeks. You're going to have to keep my hair looking good, because I cannot wash my hair in that water!"

Well, I strongly believed in answered prayer, but I wasn't too sure about a prayer of vanity. But miracle of miracles, as I went into this speaking tour, my hair continued to look as good on my last day as it did on the first without washing it.

～

Our purpose in going to Russia was to pass out Russian Bibles. We were with a tour of several physicians who brought medicine to pediatric hospitals. I remember one pediatric hospital, in poorer condition than our worst veterinary clinic in the U.S. They weren't able to have nurses, so mothers served as nurses for their children. The buildings had cracks in the walls, very little heat, were cold and drafty, and the cement outside was broken up. Mothers just had to sit there all day, and they were so grateful to have Bibles delivered personally with a smile and a genuine concern from us.

We went from room to room and gave them each a Bible. Each of the mothers took it in wonderment and would thank us. At each stop, our group shared the Bible in schools, attended teas and receptions, and press conferences. We spoke in large auditoriums, then we drove, bouncing along for eight hours in the interior of a bus with no heat. Mark found something to wrap my feet in because I was so cold.

When I spoke, I had an interpreter who would listen to me, and then speak to the audience. It was the last speaking day, when I experienced one of the most powerful events that ever happened to me in my speaking career.

As I waited for the event to begin, I sat on the platform thinking, "Wow. I almost didn't come." In the airport, as I prepared to board for this trip I remembered back that when we were briefed. The guide warned that somebody would probably be eavesdropping on all our conversations. We should be careful that we were not critical of anything, especially the KGB.

It was a good warning and it scared me to the bone. I went to the phone and called the church. Clyde was in the middle of a service and I insisted that they go and get him right off the pulpit.

"Oh, Clyde," I cried. "I can't go. I'm too frightened!"

Clyde calmly listened to my worries. Then assured me, "Gerrie, don't go then. You can come home. You don't have to go. But if you do, be safe, don't tell them about your Jewish heritage."

His comfort gave me courage and I felt relieved to go. I returned to the group and announced that I was going to go on the trip after all.

So here I sat, on that platform waiting to speak for the last time in Russia, when God showed me that this was my mission and He would protect me. On that day, on that crusade, every seat was taken and even the balcony was packed.

Mark and Lori sang, and then I was introduced. My interpreter, named Luba, stood just a foot away from me. I got up, and God just put in my heart what to say.

"I've returned to my motherland," I started. These people, who are very stoic and unaffected, surprised me when they started clapping. Then I went on to tell my story of my grandfather's escape from Russia as one of the last people to leave Minsk under the persecution of the Czar. I told how he had crawled at night, slept in the days. The Russians were listening to every word Luba spoke for me, and they were spellbound.

I told them I was so thankful that he chose freedom because it gave me the opportunity to come back and tell about my life. I told about being a young girl growing up Jewish, loving the culture, and loving my people. But then I explained that I met and fell in love with a man who was not Jewish. I went on to tell the story of how I became a Christian and how my life changed because of it.

When I was finished I saw the tears of my interpreter and I knew others were moved, too, by the countenance of those in the auditorium. They applauded and applauded, and I felt that was this was the mission God had sent me to Russia for. Even though I had spoken other places, and with success, I just knew that this was it.

Afterward a couple waited to see me. A different interpreter helped them speak to me.

The woman spoke, "Mrs. Mills, I too am Jewish," she said through the interpreter. "I do not tell this to people. My father was the very last person out of Minsk before the rest of them were slaughtered."

There was a bonding that took place between us. We chatted for quite awhile. Her husband was a gospel preacher and they'd driven hours when they'd heard that there was a Christian event planned in this city. They were so thankful they'd come, never dreaming a Jewish person would speak that day.

After I'd said good-bye to the couple, my interpreter said he wanted to talk to me alone. "Gerrie, everything you said about the atrocities that took place in Russia, are true."

I was taken aback. I said, "I'm surprised you know so much about this. I thought it would be something covered up."

He looked me right in the eye. "My mother told me," he said.

"Your mother?" I said, "Are you Jewish?"

He looked at me and didn't want to admit it. He put his finger up to his lips as if to say Shhh. He whispered, "I do not tell this because I would not have the position as an interpreter if I did. Yes, my mother is Jewish." He told me how much it meant to him that I'd shared that day.

When we got to the bus to say good-bye, people were showering us with gifts, books, and trinkets. When he and I hugged good-bye, it was my prayer that if he didn't accept the Lord Jesus this time, someone else would help him to in the future. As the bus drove out of sight, I just kept waving at him. At that moment in time I knew why God had sent me from Florida to Russia to freeze.

After two weeks, the tour was over and we were headed back to England. When the airplane landed, David, Mark, and I first ran for the candy counter in the airport and it was standing there in line when my head started to itch.

When we checked into the hotel in London, I said, "David, get the water going!" I jumped into the shower and washed my hair for a very long time. Poor David was waiting for his shower with clean water, but I didn't want to get away from the beautifully clean, fresh, water.

～

225

I was a regular speaker at the northern Michigan retreat center, Camp Barakel, where I spoke at Christian retreats, women's retreats, and children's events. They had speakers for women's retreats in the spring, four weeks in a row and fall four weeks in a row. It was one of my very favorite places to go. People who volunteered there had servants' hearts. I always felt that while I was speaking, I grew spiritually every time I went there.

Three things stand out from my experiences at Camp Barakel. One was the lowest point of my confidence as a public speaker. At Camp Barakel, I'd met a well-known Christian speaker. She had become my friend and in encouraging me to be a Christian speaker, she had critiqued my public speaking style. She was very successful and well known and I valued her opinion. She told me that I talked too much with my hands and that I should work toward being more polished and professional.

I admired her success and appreciated the time she took with me, so I was trying to speak without using my hands. But it just wasn't working well for me. My speaking felt uncomfortable to me and I felt like I was being stifled.

I'd been asked to speak at Camp Barakel, and I'd agreed, but then I learned that this friend was going to speak there, too, just one week later. I thought I couldn't possibly be on the same speaker forum as she was. I wasn't nearly as qualified as she was, and she was a wonderful Christian. Nobody would want to hear me when she would be speaking the very next week. I became very self-conscious and intimidated and didn't know if I could continue in a speaking career.

But I couldn't back out. They were counting on me. Imagine my surprise when the coordinator of the event called me to tell me that my day at the conference was full and they were redirecting all the rest of the registrants to my friend's session! That day the Lord just said, "Gerrie, start using your hands and be yourself. This is the way they remember you." It was a turning point in my speaking career.

The second thing I recall about Camp Barakel is that the lady that was in charge of the camp, Lee Hayward, expressed that the one desire in her life was that she wanted to visit Israel more than anything else in the world. I was speaking that day, and I gathered a few people at the retreat and shared Lee's desire. I asked them to see if we could make this happen over the next twenty-four hours. "Let's take Lee with us on the next tour to Israel," I suggested. Amazingly, we were able to collect the money needed for Lee's trip expenses in that twenty-four hours and presented it to her on Sunday morning. Her lifelong dream came true.

When I developed Menier's syndrome, it resulted in a significant hearing loss. A vivid memory regarding my hearing happened when I was scheduled to speak at Camp Barakel. I was living in Florida at the time. The day before I had to fly to Michigan, my hearing aid had broken. My audiologist was on vacation. What was I going to do? I was supposed to be speaking and counseling all these wonderful women for the next three days, and I couldn't do that if I couldn't hear!

A church member's son was an audiologist in Ohio. I called him, and he told me to send my broken hearing aid to him by Federal Express in Ohio. He would repair it and Fed Ex it to me at Tim and Michelle's house in Michigan. I flew in to stay with Tim and Michelle the night before the speaking event, and waited for the Fed Ex package. It didn't come.

We waited and waited until the last second before we had to leave. It was more than three hundred miles from Tim's house to Camp Barakel, and we were going to have to leave without my hearing aid.

"Lord, I need one of Your miracles," I prayed. All the girls going on the trip prayed with me, "Lord, You know what I need. Help us find the hearing aid."

We had to leave to drive the four hours to the Camp Barakel. Along the way, about forty miles from Michelle's house, we decided to stop at the McDonald's at the junction of the highway for coffee.

I kept thinking, "What am I going to do? What am I going to do?" I had to be able to hear these girls at the retreat. When we got to the McDonald's restaurant, I saw a Federal Express truck pull out of the restaurant parking lot, heading in the other direction.

I yelled, "Stop the car! That's my Fed Ex man! He's got my hearing aid, I just know it!"

Michelle, my daughter-in-law, was driving and looked at me curiously, but she stopped. "You never know," I told her as she pulled the car to the curb. Michelle thought I had lost my mind.

I almost jumped out before Michelle stopped the car. I got out, screaming, "Stop! Stop!" as I raced toward the big truck. The Federal Express driver stopped and slid his window open slightly.

"Do you happen to have a package for Gerrie Hyman Mills?" I asked him.

He gave me the strangest look. "What's your address?" he asked me, reaching for a clipboard.

It caught me off guard. I paused as I caught my breath. "I don't know. Just a minute, I'll find out."

I ran back to the car and asked Michelle, "What's my address?"

Michelle told me and I ran back to the Federal Express truck and told the driver. Sure enough! He had my hearing aid! The doctor in Ohio had put the wrong address on it, and the Fed Ex man had been trying to call me. But I wasn't listed in the book and he didn't know how to find me.

I signed for the package, grabbed it, and raced back to Michelle and the rest of the girls in the car. They were shocked and stunned. They'd thought I had been out of my mind to jump out of the car and run to a strange Fed Ex truck. But they had just seen God working, and as we headed on to Camp Barakel, Michelle and the other girls in the car marveled at the miracle they had just witnessed.

"We grew a notch in our faith today, ladies," I told the girls as I placed my hearing aid into my ear. I heard everything that day, including God's message loud and clear that He answers prayers.

Once when I was returning from another speaking engagement I experienced God's answer to prayer in a most unusual way. Instead of staying behind with the children, my friend Nancy had accompanied me that day. The winter weather was fine when we left home, but when the event was over and it was time to head home the snow was very thick and continued to blow down on us in drifts.

After a couple hours on the road, it became so intense that we couldn't see one foot in front of us; we couldn't even see the exits anymore. I said, "Nancy, we've got to pray and ask God to show us what to do."

We prayed for God to help, and all of a sudden a truck with bright headlights, running lights, and fog lights, pulled up behind us. The driver blinked his lights, and then intentionally went around us, so that we'd have lights in front of us to be able to see. He honked the horn and blinked his lights again. We followed him as closely as was safe and finally figured out between the snowflakes where the exit was. We drove off the freeway and went slipping and sliding on the exit and stopped the car. Nancy grabbed my hand and together we thanked the Lord that we made it this far and for the big truck. If truck drivers are angels, he was truly ours.

Another time, Nancy was with me when on the way home a strange car with two men in it started following us. We were trying to shake them, but they just kept following us. When I turned off the highway and they began tailgating our car on the lonely country road we knew we were in big trouble. Nancy and I were scared to death.

Nancy and I prayed, and then I said, "Hold on, Nancy!" I knew the back roads and I stepped on the gas and took off, careening around the corners on two wheels. I pulled into a hidden spot, slammed on the brakes, and turned off the headlights. Holding our breath, Nancy and I waited, and we watched the two men fly by looking for us. Again, Nancy and I thanked the Lord, waited awhile, and then drove on home safely.

While speaking was invigorating and I enjoyed sharing my story, eventually I grew tired of airports, switching planes, and the stress related to travel. It was hard leaving the family behind and trying to catch up with all of them when I returned. But recently I've begun accepting speaking engagements again and I relish the opportunity to meet new people here in California.

Chapter 34

CHRISTIANS AND JEWS UNITED

C LYDE AND I have visited Israel seven times and at the time of this writing, I am coordinating an eighth trip. Shortly after our last trip home from Israel, as Clyde and I were driving home from his hospital calls, he was thoughtful. He took my hand and squeezed it and said, "You know Gerrie, something has to be done about connecting the Jewish people and Christians. We have to show the Jewish community that the Evangelical Christians are their friends."

I shook my head in agreement, but I knew that he and I didn't know how to accomplish such a task. We would have to lean on God to make something this big happen.

We walked into the house, Clyde pressed the message machine button, and on it was an invitation for him to attend a luncheon in regards to Israel. He didn't know what, but he knew that it was definitely a leading from God.

Clyde agreed to attend the meeting, and in attending he found out there was a new movement under the leadership of John Hagee, a best-selling author, to unite the evangelical Christian and the Jewish communities.

A formal event was scheduled in Washington DC to host a gathering of members of Christians United for Israel for the purpose of introducing the association to senators and congressmen, expressing our concerns for Israel's security, and our support of Israel's right to the land by biblical mandate.

As Clyde talked with two of the leaders of this new movement at the luncheon, he responded that he was happy for this intervention for the Jewish people. After Clyde expressed his appreciation, we were both invited to a presentation by John Hagee. After the presentation, Pastor Hagee came up to us and the first thing I could think to say was, "Shalom."

I said, "Dr. Hagee, I'm Jewish," to which he replied, "I know," with a big smile on his face.

I was excited to learn there soon would be a similar event in Sacramento. Plans were being made to go to Washington for the first Israel summit to meet with senators and congressmen, and stand on the steps of the nation's capital with thousands of others in support of Israel. I knew that as much as I desired to go, I probably would not be able to afford it. It has been my lifelong dream to unite Jews and Christians for the cause of Israel.

An email came saying that three thousand people were signed up to attend the Stand for Israel. Depressed, I looked at Clyde and told him, "It should have been 3001."

Clyde looked at me kindly and said, "Gerrie, if you feel you need to go, I want you to go."

I did want to go, with all my heart. I wanted to be the first one to stand up for Israel and all my people. Our church made it possible, by paying for all my expenses to go, but then I learned that the convention was not taking any more registrations. It couldn't be 3001 after all.

I called my friend Victor to tell him that I could go, and he told me the event was filled to capacity. He told me, "Pray Gerrie, just pray. Put your faith to work and we'll see."

Victor called one of the secretaries that worked for the John Hagee organization. He explained that I wanted to go, and was given the answer, "Wait and see."

A few days later, Victor called me back, "Gerrie, you are the last human being to be able to attend the Washington summit. They are making an exception for you." God had a plan, and I was able to attend this historical event.

While I was in Washington Victor told Clyde that he and Marita would take responsibility for me. That was the nicest thing, and I was given access to special dignitaries, the press conference, and other events that I could never had done on my own. Victor Styrsky is one of the sweetest Christian men that God has raised up to make this Christians Untied for Israel powerful, and he is being used to speak in the Jewish communities throughout the U.S.

Even though I was just one small person, I was honored to take my stand before God and the United States to stand up as a Jewish Christian in public support of the Jewish people. I wanted to represent my church and my community in Sun City Lincoln Hills.

Standing there that day was such a sense of gratification that the church had sent me. As each of the senators and congressmen echoed my sentiments of my feelings of support, I felt the power of God working throughout that crowd of thousands.

I returned to Sacramento to report back. I wanted to do all I could to further the cause. A conference was planned in Sacramento at a big theater, to bring the Jewish community to tell them how much we evangelicals have appreciated all the Jewish people.

Al Kline was the Shalom Group president in Sun City, and when we approached him he was apprehensive, thinking it would be Christian preaching. But when Clyde assured him that was not the purpose, and that the event was endorsed by the Jewish Federation, it was approved. Our church hired two large buses and took everybody in the Jewish community who wanted to go in Sun City to the event. We bought all the tickets we could, and the event sold out.

Afterward, the Jewish people who attended couldn't thank us enough and they still tell us it was one of the most outstanding nights of their lives.

I felt good about participating because it demonstrated my loyalty to Israel, and the cause for Israel. I am a Jew and I am a Christian, yet I will always treasure my Jewish heritage.

AFTERWORD

So, that's my story.

A lifetime of ministry as a pastor's wife who is Jewish. There have been many, many more unmentioned day-to-day miracles, holy encounters, and people who have touched my life along the way. I believe that God chooses people to place in my path for me to love and serve.

My ministry has always been about linking God with people. The blessings of walking with the Lord each day are countless and it's such a good deal. How else can you have eternal life for free?

You can be certain of your salvation today—just call on Jesus. You will be amazed at how quickly He answers your prayer. Jesus loves you and He is just waiting to hear from you.

I would not want to end my story without sharing that life-changing opportunity:

> *Dear Jesus,*
>
> *I understand that I can have eternal life by believing that You died on the cross and rose from the dead to forgive me of my sins. I know that I need You, and I invite You to come into my life. I welcome You as my Savior and Lord. Help me to be the kind of person You want me to be.*
>
> *Amen.*

Such a deal.

NOTES

Chapter 12

1. Oswald Chambers, *My Utmost for His Highest* (Grand Rapids, MI: Discovery House Publishers, 1935) p. 64.

Chapter 19

1. "104th Anniversary for local church," *The Coldwater Daily Reporter*, Coldwater, Michigan, from the early 1970s.

To Contact the Author

WWW.GERRIEHYMANMILLS.COM